SAY IT LOUD...
I Sell And I'm Proud

SAY IT LOUD...
I Sell And I'm Proud

◆

A CAREER PROSPECTUS

Tyrone L. Cypress

iUniverse, Inc.
New York Lincoln Shanghai

SAY IT LOUD...I Sell And I'm Proud
A CAREER PROSPECTUS

iUniverse books may be ordered through booksellers or by contacting:

iUniverse
2021 Pine Lake Road, Suite 100
Lincoln, NE 68512
www.iuniverse.com
1-800-Authors (1-800-288-4677)

ISBN-13: 978-0-595-38050-3 (pbk)
ISBN-13: 978-0-595-82420-5 (ebk)
ISBN-10: 0-595-38050-6 (pbk)
ISBN-10: 0-595-82420-X (ebk)

Printed in the United States of America

Contents

IT FINALLY GOT THE BEST OF ME

Okay, that's it! I've had it! In my almost 30 years of professional selling, I've endured the subtle put downs and negative characterizations of my chosen profession.

"We'll get started momentarily, and we will do our best to avoid sounding like Salespeople."

Did you hear him? I'm telling you, it borders on slander.

The good doctor (Ph. D. type), who serves as the technical lead for a major Information Security company, invited us to this palatial exhibition hall in downtown Washington, D.C. to see a presentation of his company's latest computer security products and services.

How dare he begin the session with that comment to a room full of Salespeople! Especially when you consider that the reason for this gathering is to convince us to become "RESELLERS."

Well Doc, if you're so smart, why do you need our help?

Why does there seem to be so little appreciation and respect for what we do? I know, I know! After all these years you would think that I would be unscathed by such a remark. What's gotten into me? Why am I so exercised?

I need to vent. The doctor's quip has served as the proverbial "straw."

"How", you ask? Consistent with the traditional ways of a professional Salesperson, where discretion being the better part of valor, going out of the way not to offend, and by all means avoiding a confrontation, the answer—WRITE A BOOK!

This is my attempt at telling it like it is (as I see it)[1] with the staunch conviction of a grateful participant. My effort is not intended to be a "how to", but a "how come". And, I'll take extra care not to sound like an apologist trying to make excuses for a lack-luster career. Selling is not easy. It is a demanding profession even for the gifted, but the rewards can be euphoric. I can't imagine doing anything else. Our profession is the ultimate "bootstrap" scenario where your limits are your own doing. Think it, do it, and do it again (author privilege).

Early in my career I came to realize that nothing happens in an organization if nothing is sold. It is what makes the business world go-round. Every department, every division, and every function of an organization, as well as the corporate well being of ALL its employees and shareholders, depends on Sales. Did you hear that? There is no aspect of a company more important to its continued existence than its Sales force (no matter how that effort is comprised). For the non-believers let me illuminate the point: **SELL OR PERISH!**

In the midst of all the peaks and valleys like a mantra in a phrase—SAY IT LOUD, I SELL AND I'M PROUD.

---

1. Now, please keep in mind that I was drawn into this endeavor as a means of getting it off my chest. I have harbored most of these thoughts for a long time. In an attempt to present my experiences without offending specific individuals or companies, I have intentionally changed certain locations, specific times, and taken great care to invoke certain people and events as amalgams and aliases.

OH, THE SHAME OF IT ALL

The social branding of our profession is pretty wide spread. We are held in low esteem by a large segment of the population—lower than attorneys and almost as low as politicians. I have heard enough of the bad jokes and putdowns to get the point. I have heard the utterances ranging from the "sales job" that took place in the Garden of Eden, right up to and including modern day descriptions and depictions of "bait-and-switch" sales tactics seen on T.V. The smears seem to be old and wide reaching.

Confidence man (conman), snake oil salesman, used car salesman, pitchman, commissioned salesman, shark, traveling salesman, front man, door-to-door salesman, peddler, head hunter, and these are just a few of the double entendres and negative aspersions prevalent in the day-to-day glossary of terms used to identify Salespeople and their behavior.

"No Salesman will call."

"This is the truth, not a sales pitch."

"Our agents are consultants, not Salespeople."

Harmless? Not on your life. These are representations of the accepted defamations found in our cultural lexicon that go unchallenged even by Salespeople. Over the years I have noticed that most Salespeople shy away from the very title of "Salesman." Shame, shame. For example, just take a look at the business cards of any group of people that sell for a living. You might expect the title to read Salesperson, or Sales Representative, but in my experience I have found almost *every other title or label under the sun*: Account Representative/Executive, Business Developer, Marketing Representative/Executive/Associate, Consultant, Major Account Representative, Channel Marketing Representative, Territory Manager, Special Events Coordinator, Specialist, and on and on—choosing anything to keep away from being identified as a Salesperson.

If you have some direct responsibility for sales, whether you are commissioned or not, the word "SALES" should appear on your business card! It is okay to use words like Senior, Executive, National, Regional, and District in some combination with the word "SALES" for flavoring, but do not avoid the word entirely. My goodness, it seems as though we are "in denial."

...AND MORE SHAME

A co-worker once relayed the following story to me:

She and her husband were invited by her sister to attend a small gathering of friends, but her sister would not reveal the reason for the invitation.

Somewhat suspicious of the secrecy, my coworker asked her sister, "Is this an Amway session?"

"No," replied her sister.

What's so bad about selling Amway? Although, many of the people attempting to sell these products do not thoroughly understand the business principles of the programs, I always thought Amway, Shaklee, and some of the other multi-level marketing concepts were solid business opportunities.

As it turned out, it was an Amway meeting. Ouch! My coworker said she could hardly contain herself during the meeting. When it was over she confronted her sister and to her amazement her sister showed no remorse. She was not the least bit sorry for the deception. In fact, her sister seemed quite pleased with herself. The ends justified the means. She was so convinced of the merits of the program she felt she had done no wrong. At least that was her story. My coworker on the other hand was so put off by the ordeal that the relationship between the sisters suffered irreversible damage.

What's the lesson here? I don't think the Amway Rep was nearly as sure of herself and comfortable with her tactics as she espoused. You should not have to deliberately mislead your audience or prospects to make an offer of a legitimate business proposition. The problem as I saw it was that she was afraid of being a Salesperson. I am not suggesting that this is the standard M.O. for Amway, and my recounting this story is not meant to slam Amway at all, but I have heard a number of similar circumstances (not to mention my own personal encounters) involving multilevel marketing that justify my conclusion—they try to disguise the fact that they are Salespeople.

Salespeople take a stand! It is time that we stop allowing these misperceptions of what we do to drive us to these unseemly shenanigans. Just stop it!

SILLY WILLY

I remember having a discussion with a colleague who was inspired by the movie *Glengarry Glen Ross*. My colleague remarked that this was "The Movie." The most profound story ever about how it is in the real world and although dramatized for entertainment value, it was really on the mark. It was gritty, raw, and brutally honest. She just went on and on recanting one terrific scene after another.

"Now this is the way Salespeople are viewed by the world," she went on. "This puts it all into perspective. Don't you agree?"

Whoa! What are you saying? If this group of salesmen represents an accurate portrayal of "real world" sales professionals, no wonder we are viewed with such disdain. Although I agreed that it was a great movie, it might be one of the few movies with no good guys. (Not among the major characters. The salesmen were a bunch of scoundrels. In my opinion, it was the artful dialogue and the dynamic acting performances that greatly contributed to why the movie was so moving and captivating.)

As I further explained, in what probably seemed to be a didactic retort, the story I point to for perspective is *Death of a Salesman*. My colleague was not impressed.

"Huh? You're kidding, right? Talk about hanging crepe, Tyrone. I really think you should broaden your horizons."

"Well now, just hear me out," I said spontaneously. "As you know, for a number of years I have contended that when it comes to how Salespeople are perceived in society, we are in large measure the culprits, mainly due to the fact that our perspective is skewed, just like Willy Loman's."

Arthur Miller wrote about the neurotic state of Willy Loman as he was enraptured into becoming a success, but it's Willy's perception of success that begets my point. Willy saw success only as material success. He convinced his family members, especially his sons, that their perspectives must coincide with his. As the plot thickens, Willy also thinks that his family cannot love him unless he is successful. Willy was so consumed with this notion of success that he condoned dishonesty and thievery as a means to an end. Ben (Willy's brother) and Linda (Willy's wife) were symbolic as two opposing forces represented in Willy's quagmire. Ben was a material success void of any loving qualities. Linda loved Willy unconditionally and did not share Willy's view of success. In Willy's mind, love was not possible without success.

Without going through the back and forth of each character's interplay, I will suffice it to say that with all of these contradictions fueling Willy's obsessions, he never truly realized success. He convinced himself that he was a failure and committed suicide before he could figure out why. *Death of a Salesman* is a masterful depiction of contrasting influences, but for me, the moral is clear—SUCCESS, ETHICS AND ESTEEM ARE SUBJEC-TIVE OBJECTIVES.

Our profession affords us meaningful success at many levels. Although I have the utmost respect for the Salespeople at the top of the ladder, I submit to you that you don't have to rise to the stature of Tony Robbins or Zig Ziegler to proclaim success. Aspire all you want, climb that ladder, ride that wave, sales is a profession that provides for meritorious achievement, but remember "Silly Willy." You set the watermark, you make the call. Do not permit social conditioning to dictate the measurement of who you are and what you do within our profession.

ON YOUR MARK, GET SET...

Here is the way it all started for me...

It was the summer of '68 while working as an Intelligence Clerk for the Defense Intelligence Agency in Washington, D.C. when I decided to go to college. This decision was precipitated by a number of career "pass-overs" and "pass-arounds". I was consistently told that it was the lack of a college degree that stood in the way of any significant career advancements or promotions. My Navy training and experience didn't seem to matter. Without a degree, I simply could not escape the ranks of the non-professional billets. My coworkers, the ones with degrees, seemed to be getting promoted at a lightning pace. So, I began investigating some local schools, and after some due diligence in determining how to afford it all, I chose Howard University.

I actually started at Howard in September 1969. For me, attending school part-time was not an option. I knew from the beginning that I had to jump in head-on and complete the process as soon as possible—not allowing the many possible distractions to interfere. This meant leaving DIA and attending school on a full-time basis.

Goodbye civil service—Hello real world. What on Earth was I thinking? Due diligence? I hadn't thought this whole thing through at all. I merely convinced myself that it was doable and affordable, because I wanted it so badly.

Although the GI Bill certainly helped, additional monies were needed, if I was going to get though this endeavor. Eventually, I ended up working two jobs while carrying a full load (18 credit hours) so I could graduate in four years. (By the way, I later applied for and received a Board of Trustees Academic Scholarship, which also helped to defray some of the costs).

Now I am on my way—destined to be a Political Science student eager for the challenges. Choosing Political Science was a natural. I was a teen of the '60s, full of the images and rhetoric of the times. Not to mention that I was a Vietnam era veteran who had also worked for DIA and CIA. It all seemed so clear.

But there was another wrinkle. It seemed as though practically every freshman at Howard that year also wanted to enroll in Political Science. All of the Political Science courses filled while I bounced from one line to another trying to squeeze into any of the posted classes. The campus chatter was that a number of Business courses were open and students were enrolling in them to fill up their schedules. It certainly seemed to be the thing to do at the time. So, I did.

Little did I know what a life altering effect this would have on my career.

The Business courses were outstanding. I particularly liked the teaching method of bringing successful business people from the community into the classroom for face-to-face student conferences and seminars.

And, then it happened. One day in marketing class, an Insurance Salesman was brought in to address the students. He was specifically summoned to establish Professional Sales as a legitimate career choice for our consideration. This was no small feat. Many of the students (including me) thought of Salesmen as "hustlers", not businessmen.

I was extremely impressed and affected by him and what he had to say. I was so swayed by his message and his delivery; he made me feel like a groupie. By the end of the class I wanted to look like him, talk like him, walk like him, act like him, dress like him...And, what's really remarkable is as impressed as I was with this gentleman, today I can't recall his name or the company for which he worked.

I made up my mind the next day to change my major. The next semester I was immersed in the Business curriculum, and never once thought about studying Political Science again.

I found all of my business courses to be challenging and interesting. Call me crazy, but I enjoyed courses like Small Business Management, Production Management and Managerial Economics. I particularly liked the Marketing courses. Marketing proved to be the gateway to understanding Merchandising—a concept that I found to be at the very foundation of professional selling. Gantt charts, Program Evaluation Review Technique (PERT) charts, Critical Path Method (CPM)...I was becoming armed to take on the world.

I would be less than honest if I pretended that it all came so easily. College Business Math proved to be a monster. First of all, it was obvious that the math courses in high school had not prepared me for the onslaught of Howard's Business curriculum. Calculus I and II, Statistics, and Quantitative Analysis proved to be about all I could handle. To further complicate matters, my Calculus instructors were from India and spoke with very heavy accents. Can you imagine taking a subject as difficult as Calculus and not being able to understand the instructor?

THIS SEEMS LIKE A GOOD PLACE TO START

Off to IBM Sales School in Dallas, Texas—Not so fast.

At IBM there were some prerequisites to Sales School. In fact, my initial interview for the Sales position is worth revisiting.

I was recommended for the interview by the senior administrator I reported to while working part-time as an equipment installer in D.C. He was impressed with my work ethic and arranged for me to talk with the Branch Manager. Nervous and excited, I showed up for the interview one hour early and waited for the Branch Manager to return from lunch. I simply could not wait to get started.

The Secretary, whose desk was in the waiting area, could not take her eyes off of me. At the time I thought that it might have been because I was so "irresistible." (I was dressed to kill. I had on a black, well-fitting suit with white piping and a pair of white patent-leather shoes.) Today, I realize that the Secretary's stares were not because of my charm but because she probably thought I was one of the Temptations. You would think that after working part-time at IBM for more than two years, I might have gotten the word about the "dress code" for business attire, particularly the infamous IBM dress code: a dull, blue or gray, ill-fitting suit (two or three piece) with 16 pound wingtips, and of course, a plain white shirt accented only by a red or maroon silk tie. Frankly, I am not sure what got into me, except to say that I have always tended to overdress. I did not come to appreciate conservative, custom-made clothing until much later in my professional career.

No matter, the Branch Manager did not seem phased at all. Luckily, he made up his mind to hire me before the interview even took place, based on the Administrator's recommendation—not to mention that IBM had just instituted some very stringent Affirmative Action hiring initiatives. That's right...and I'm not ashamed to admit it. I was probably hired because of Affirmative Action. If I had not worked my butt off and proven myself though, I would not have been there very long.

I was assigned to the Bethesda, Maryland commercial office—an office of one Branch Manager, four Marketing Managers and 30+ Sales Reps—four of us very newly hired. We were required to undergo six weeks of rigorous in-branch product training. During that period, we spent from four to six hours per day practicing and refining our demonstration skills. There was no shortage of products on which to practice. At that time the Office Products Division offered Typewriters, Copiers, and Dictation Equipment (several types of each) with complimenting supplies. You got it—we were even taught how to "pitch" supplies.

Although interesting and fun-filled, in-branch training proved to be somewhat grueling. There was a lot to learn and IBM's expectations were high. Training culminated with a final stand-up demonstration of a selected product in front of the entire office at a Branch Office Meeting. I "lucked out." I drew the IBM Correcting Selectric Typewriter, which was one of the most demonstrable products ever. I conferred with the Senior Reps in the office and carefully wrote the script, and then I painstakingly memorized every word. I had never been so prepared for anything in my life. The time that I put in paid off in spades. The demo went extremely well. I can still remember how proud I was when the Senior Reps congratulated me afterwards—saying things like, "That's one of the best..."; "We didn't realize you were so talented..."; "You're a natural..."; and "You are going to knock 'em dead in Dallas." (How 'bout them Affirmative Action apples?) I guess we all like the adoration of our peers, but this *sealed the deal* for me. If I had not already been committed to a sales career, I was now.

J. C. ▮▮▮▮▮
8401 Connecticut Avenue, Chevy Chase, Maryland 20015
September 1, 1977

Dear Tyrone,

I know that 1977 has been a particularly exciting and challenging year with new product announcements and the OP/OS marketing direction and you've stepped up to that challenge.

I appreciate all your effort and success - but we don't want to overlook another important area of the business—supplies. Supplies in 1977 could potentially provide a significant portion of your annual compensation.

With your sales ability, technical knowledge and our comprehensive service and distribution, we feel that we can compete favorably for Supplies business and enlist your support in doing so.

Our primary marketing strategy is to sell Supply Agreements with Supply Kit Sales as a secondary strategy when equipment is being ordered.

In reviewing the unreconciled June Supply Sales Record Summary, I see that you've sold $28,841 in Supplies and are 192% of quota year-to-date through June. Thank you! However, I wonder if you're aware that you could have earned potentially $280 MORE in Supplies commissions? $9,337 of your total supplies billed was not through Supply Agreements or Supply Kits, and, therefore, was not eligible for the three percent bonus.

Last year, a total of 37 percent of our Supplies revenue was sold through Supply Agreements. We would like to increase considerably our Supply Agreement and Supply Kit Sales in 1977. You can help us in achieving that objective — and earning significant supplies commissions for yourself.

Thank you - and good selling!

Very truly yours,

Joe

Mr. Tyrone L. Cypress
Bethesda Branch

(Illustration I)

NOW, OFF TO SCHOOL...

It did not take long for me to realize why the IBM Sales School was so highly regarded. Although they were courteous, respectful and professional, they were *boot planting* the entire time. They pushed us to the max of our capabilities and capacities.

There was one particular water hazard called "Rotate and Demonstrate." This event called for seven demonstrations on seven different products, one following immediately after the other. A combination of rooms and cubicles were used to separate the settings where an instructor sat on one side of the product and role-played the customer. You were given a certain number of minutes, depending on the product, to go in and set the stage by way of questioning techniques, and to get a commitment from the customer to start the demo. Performing the demo was not a given; you had to earn the right. The theme of the demo process was Feature-Function-Benefit. Identify the features, discuss their functionality, and relate the precise benefits to the customer. Oh yea, did you ask for the order? After each demo the instructor would critique you, pointing out the good and the bad, and then mete out a score ranging from one to four—four being the best. They would also rate your performance with a "SALE" or "NO SALE", i.e., 2=No Sale, 3=Sale. Seem easy? Sounds fair enough, but you would not believe the consternation caused by this phase of the training. The instructors were unmerciful if you did not ask for the order. You would also encounter their wrath if you continued to talk once you had the commitment for the sale.

I stayed at a hotel across the street from the training facility where there was a room set up as a Chapel for the guests. Since I had to pass this area going to and from my room, I could not help but notice when it was being used. Each night before the "Rotate and Demonstrate" sessions, the students would line the halls and wait for an opportunity to avail themselves of the Chapel to pray for divine help in getting through the process.

One might have thought that for me, Sales School would have been a breeze with all that "natural ability" and all. Not so. I struggled through practically every phase of training. There was more to Sales Training than being a good "pitchman." There was so much to learn.

I'M NOT WORTHY?

I often reflect back on a situation I had with one of the instructors that jolted my professional senses. Roughly, here's what happened:

The class was asked to select four classmates to be nominated for the "Top Rep" honor. I was one of the nominees. The class then cast their votes by writing their selection on a small piece of paper and passing it forward. The four nominees were asked to cast their votes and then wait in the hallway while the votes were being tallied and preparations were being made to announce the winner. As it turned out there was a two-way tie, and I was one of the chosen. During the recounting process, one of the instructors discovered that I had not voted for myself. In other words, had I done so, I would have won the honor. I will never forget the look on that instructor's face. He called me back out into the hallway and like a drill instructor he lit into me.

He started by saying, "Don't you ever."

That's when all of my defensive apparatus went up, blocking out most of what followed, but I got the message. He removed my name from further consideration. Oddly enough and for a long time after that, I could not see what was so terribly wrong in what I had done. However, over the years I have come to realize why it was important to have voted for myself. Especially since I was nominated by others in the group and given their vote of confidence.

All in all, Sales School proved to be a good first step in my development as a professional salesman. I guess they prepared me as best they could for my first territory, considering it was Prince George's County, Maryland—not exactly a Metropolis in the early to mid '70s.

TRAINING...THE GUIDING LIGHT

In my career I have been fortunate to go through some excellent training courses. I am convinced that professional training is absolutely necessary to be competitive in the world of professional sales. If you have not received some, go get some and, no matter how much you have had, go get some more. I look at it as an on-going process. I have found that all of the sales training programs of which I have been involved (Needs Satisfaction, PSS, and SPIN) have paid off in huge dividends over the years and helped me through many selling escapades.

NEEDS SATISFACTION: At the root of Needs Satisfaction is something called Homeostasis. Its premise is that in order to sell someone you must first upset their status quo and make them uncomfortable with the way things are then show them how your product or service improves the condition. Usually, sales professionals are calling on prospects that have not asked for a sales quote or a presentation. That is where these fundamentals have some real merit. Here is one of the role plays that we used at the IBM Sales School to illustrate the point:

The exercise was called "Sell Me Something; Sell Me Anything." An instructor dressed and posed as a wealthy carpet merchant who was in his office going about his daily routine. He was not wearing shoes; he was smoking and depositing his ashes on a very expensive carpet beneath his chair. Smoke filled the room and seemed to cause him a great deal of discomfort. The carpet merchant also let it be known that sales were off and his pet dog, which lay at his feet, seemed to be ill all the time.

The students were asked to presume that they had gotten past the Secretary and were now talking to the carpet merchant in an attempt to sell him anything; sell him something. One after the other we took our shots. It was amazing how we missed the big picture. We went straight for the obvious. We tried preaching about the evils of smoking, the expense of replacing things in his office, the improvement to the environment, global warming (which was a real stretch in the early '70s), etc. We were all over the place. This simple exercise was full of lessons and pointed out just how amateurish we were and why the awareness of a selling strategy was so crucial.

The instructor masterfully took us through the calls. Replacing expensive carpets was no problem; he was wealthy. He was unsure why his sales were off. (He suspected it had something do with a comment he overheard a customer make about the inventory having an odor of something burning.) His pet dog was allowed in the office because he was thought of as a member of the family. What's the big deal about bare feet? Little by little we were shown how the right questioning techniques could uncover well-hidden and unrealized reasons to change.

What products and/or services would you sell the carpet merchant? How? Why? We spent the better part of a full class day on this exercise. Once we got the hang of it we were unstoppable. We found the numbers of products and services that we could sell the carpet merchant were nearly infinite.

> Mr. Carpet Merchant, you mentioned that you were very concerned that your pet dog was in bad health. Did you know our statistics show that a dog's life may be extended dramatically while living in a smoke free environment? Since we have concluded that you will never be able to stop smoking, what if I could show you a way to improve your dog's health, thereby extending his life expectancy, while you continue to smoke? Would you be interested in such a product or service? Our air conditioning and climate control...

I could write chapter after chapter detailing this exercise and our discoveries of that day, but suffice it to say, you must find out what's important, and why, and use that information to affect a change.

<u>PSS:</u> Professional Selling Skills (PSS) I found to be slightly different. I am not sure if I experienced the real PSS, but the company I was working for at the time, told us that their training method was PSS. (In comparison

to what a number of my friends who worked with other companies, i.e., Xerox, had experienced, I found that our notes did not jive.) As we were taught, PSS places a lot of emphasis on identifying and isolating the characteristics of the decision makers and the influencers. PSS contends that there are four basic types of decision makers:

The CONTROLLER is the ultimate authority who insists on being involved and in control of every aspect of the decision making process. He or she usually dominates the conversation and likes to give orders.

The PROMOTER is outgoing, gregarious, almost braggadocios. His or her products are the greatest ever and nothing compares. He is Mr. "Glad Hand"; always the schmoozer; the life of the party; the master of ceremony.

The ANALYZER is a nerd, susceptible to analysis paralysis. He cloaks himself in a mountain of details and buries every decision under a ton of minutia. He or she tends to be extremely anal and is undoubtedly a salesman's worst nightmare.

The SUPPORTER is the consummate follower. His or her decision criterion is always attached to the welfare or impacts the status of others.

Now, the above assertions are in the extreme. No one is a pure encasement of these traits. Most decision makers seem to have some elements of each trait—different characteristics appear depending on the type of decision being made: business; personal; social; etc. All that being said, this is a real phenomenon. The time I spent learning this concept has paid off enormously. I'll avoid turning this section into a tutorial on decision making characteristics, but I would like to share the one little factoid derived from this concept that has been ingrained into my business and social conscience—CROSS-TRAITS CLASH!

CONTROLLER	PROMOTER
ANALYZER	SUPPORTER

Controllers clash with Supporters (and vice-versa) and Promoters clash with Analyzers (and vice-versa). This is a bit-o-truth that has been borne out over the life of my professional selling career. Once I identify the frame of reference to which I am dealing, at all costs I avoid appearing like the cross-trait.

The traits on the upper level of the chart tend to be people in charge, and the traits on the lower level tend to be influencers, but they rarely have the final say-so.

I have found this technique particularly useful in the interviewing process—both as the interviewer and the interviewee. When I am looking to hire a Sales Rep, I am looking for a Promoter, faults and all. When applying for a job, knowing which character type is sitting in front of me really gives me an edge. Since my style tends to be that of a Promoter, when I am engaging an Analyzer, I immediately morph into the Controller or Supporter trait.

Initially, I did not think there was much to this selling method. However, I have done a complete turnaround on this strategy. We were told that Madison Avenue packages their advertisements and promotions based on this concept. We were even shown training films made by famous athletes where they showed how the technique was used to recruit high school and college athletes to their programs. Since studying the techniques, I am now almost immediately able to detect which character trait a commercial message is targeting. Within moments, I can tell which category a prospect falls into during a sales call.

Can you say V_ _ _ _? There is no doubt in my mind who their car-buying target audience is. Test yourself. The next time you hear a commercial; see if you can discern if there is a targeted audience being addressed. The really good ones will touch on more than one of them.

<u>SPIN:</u> At the time I was introduced to SPIN it was touted as a questioning technique that was designed to elicit both the customer's apparent and hidden buying motives and objectives.

S-Situation
P-Problem
I-Implication
N-Need (payoff)

Today SPIN has evolved into more than just a questioning technique. It is currently being used by a number of companies as their primary (and sometimes only) selling method.

DO THE MATH

<u>VALUE PROPOSITION:</u> Why it is necessary to expound on the value added aspects of the products and a Sales Rep's trump card. Being able to competently discuss profitability and Return on Investment (ROI). It seems as though I've had some fable-like encounters on the job that brought to light the significance of the Value Proposition. Check this out...

There was a large grocery chain headquartered in my territory that drew a number of Reps and vendors to their door trying to peddle their corporate wares. In fact, there were several IBM Reps calling on this account. I was pushing Office Products, but there must have been at least three IBM Reps representing the Computer Division (I didn't know any of them and we were all in different offices). I called the head of procurement, introduced myself as the new IBM Sales Rep, and asked for an appointment to come out and briefly meet. We had just announced several new products and I could hardly wait to present them.

"Okay," he said, "When you get here, sign in at the lobby entrance and I'll come down to get you."

The day of the appointment I arrived to a shocking visual. The lobby was a big open space, about 22' x 22', with chairs lined up next to one another all around the room. Every chair was filled with a Rep waiting their turn to speak to someone in the purchasing department. The line continued out the door. There must have been 100 Reps waiting.

I approached the receptionist behind the glass window and announced, "I'm Tyrone Cypress from IBM." (with a little more volume on I-B-M.) "Would you let Mr. So-and-So know that I'm here for our appointment?"

"Okay, he'll be down shortly," she replied. "Please have a seat."

There were no empty seats and I was not about to go outside and stand in line. I was with IBM and that's gotta buy me something.

After what seemed like an eternity of standing in the middle of the room and waiting for the Procurement Manager, I finally decided to mingle. I discovered that the Reps lining the walls were Stocking Reps. They were waiting for the opportunity to obtain shelving space in the stores to stock their products for sale.

I engaged one of the Reps, "How about this line?"

"Well, actually the line is moving pretty fast today."

Good grief, this is normal? One of the Reps asked me if I was from IBM and before I knew it I was heading into a four or five Sales Rep conversation about selling to the grocery chain. These guys had the patience of Jobe and really knew their stuff. One of them mentioned that he knew of one of the IBM Reps that was calling on the grocery chain. He said the Rep had a new product that was going to revolutionize how business was conducted in grocery stores across the Country.

"Wow," I said. "How so?"

"Well," he continued, "It's a scanner. You simply wave each item across a small window at the checkout counter and it automatically records and tallies your purchase."

"Oh, my! That's very impressive," I exclaimed. But actually, the full impact of this revelation was a mere glancing blow. I didn't get it. This was revolutionary? Although I was not aware of this device, I was aware of barcode scanning, and I just could not see how that was going to be such a big deal. Don't let anyone accuse me of having foresight or being a visionary...

The conversation continued. It was like a sales seminar—an eye-opener. Finally, I was beginning to see the big picture. Not only would this speed up the lines, but it would also affect inventory, stocking, replenishing, and reordering. Deliveries would be affected. Prices could be lowered. Productivity would be increased. Before long, we had revamped the entire operation of the chain and every vendor that called on them. One of the Reps started to talk about how the chain's profitability would be affected.

Here is the lesson of the day. Can you guess what the profit margin is for the average grocery store?

   A. 50%

   B. 25%

   C. 15%

   D. 10%

   E. <1%

Everybody in the conversation seemed to know, but me. The Answer: F. Less than 1%. That meant for every dollar of revenue being generated from sales, less than one penny was profit. Basically there are only two ways to increase profits: (1) Increase Sales; or (2) Reduce Costs.

It didn't take me long to figure out how far I could go with this story. Armed with this information about the grocery chain, coupled with the ability to relate the profitability story, I was prepared to sell them most anything. This approach allowed for the cost justification of even some of my more expensive products.

Just think of the compelling case you could make to a decision maker:

> *Mr. DM, my products can significantly effect nearly every phase of your operation by dramatically reducing your cost of doing business. I project that we could save your organization about 25% on the planned equipment purchase alone.*

Most top-level decision makers are quick to pick up on this point. It seems that the higher the executive on the Org Chart, the more in-tune they are to this rationale. A company with a 1% profit margin would have to generate a million dollars worth of sales revenue to have the same effect on profitability as reducing operation costs by $10,000.00. In other words, $10,000.00 in cost reductions = $1,000,000.00 in sales revenue.

Of course, the other IBM Reps already knew this and were able to sell millions of dollars worth of products and services to the store. Incidentally, I didn't do too badly myself. I handled this account for about two years, and remember reading a year or so after moving on to another territory, that this grocery chain had one of the highest profit margins in their industry across the Country—about 15%!

HONING, TONING, SPYING AND BEGUILING

I guess one of the most captivating aspects of a professional sales career is how the demands of the profession force you to draw from all of your talents. In order to successfully compete in a multitude of arenas against a large number of highly competent Sales Reps and volatile economies with dips and dives in customer consumption, Sales Reps are compelled to call on their training, background and natural abilities to endure.

One of my safety nets has always been to immerse myself in the various trade rags about sales methodologies and skill development. Even after all these years of selling I spend a lot of time reading about success stories and sales concepts. I enjoy sales seminars and workshops as much as a good movie or play. I find the motivational tapes to be both inspirational as well as educational. These are some of the ways I have been able to establish the foundation for carrying out my day-to-day approach to selling. Continually enhancing my skills in the basic areas such as: Proposal Writing and Presentations; Overcoming Objections; Creating a 'Value Proposition'; Qualifying Prospects; and Developing Closing Techniques, a.k.a. Selling is Fundamental.

Now, as committed as I am toward perfecting my skills at this level, I am acutely aware that this is not all that is necessary to survive in the dog-eat-dog world of professional sales. Because sales opportunities are so situational, I have found that flexibility is also an important aspect of successful selling—there is nothing quite like having an ear or nose for selling. Some of the best Salespeople with whom I have had the chance to work, all seemed to have had an uncanny sense of finding opportunities and knowing just how to seek out and address the customer's real buying criteria.

Early in my career and for a number of years, I spent a lot of time searching for ways to improve my natural abilities. I finally concluded that natural abilities are just that—natural. Although some have more than others, you either have them or you don't. For me the only payoffs resulting in this area were the lessons learned during the daily challenges while in the heat of battle—On the Job Training.

Truth is we all seem to be in a constant state of honing the process. We talk about it. We read about it. We leap headlong at every opportunity to implore it.

STRATEGICALLY YOURS

An imperative task of a Sales professional is developing the strategies to maximize the resources and effectively employ the capabilities of their organization. In theory, this is a pretty basic concept; however, in reality the challenges are enormous. It's another one of those factors that separates Professional Sales from mere clerking.

It would be fairly simple to sell a product or service if it was the biggest, fastest, cheapest, etc., and ready for instant delivery at no additional charge. However, I have yet to encounter this circumstance. My experience has always been that something was lacking. After all, that's why you need Salespeople. That's why Salespeople need a sales strategy—to overcome the objections to the missing elements of your offering. Oh yea, there's one other important reason for a Salesperson—to maximize the profits of the sales transaction. The initial responsibility for establishing the worth of the goods sold and then being able to close the deal at that price is that of the Sales Rep. Leave no money on the table and convince the customer that they got a great deal. Can you say "Value Proposition"?

I have found that strategizing my approach to the sales effort on the fly serves as a check and balance for evaluating whether I am making a sincere attempt at trying to secure the business. Did I present the product/service in its best light? Did I fully understand the product/service and how it really stacked up to the competition? Am I knocking on enough doors? Am I giving the opportunity the full benefit of my experience?

I often asked myself if the company or the boss was paying me enough to sell the goods, but I also thought to ask myself—was I earning the money I was being paid to push the goods? I am sure if I was not earning the money they wouldn't have paid me for very long, but the question served to urge me along. In other words, is this a stratagem or a day-at-the-gym?

Relying on the base concepts has always served me well—trying not to stray from the universal buying criteria. As you can imagine, there are many nuances involved in creating a competitive, professional sales strategy and I generally approach each opportunity on a case-by-case basis, weaving through and around the obstacles with the basics:

-Reduce Costs (Cost Justify)

-Increase Productivity (Process Improvements)

-Scrutinize the Org Chart (Responsibility for Cost Savings and Product Enhancements)

-Know What They Have and WHAT THEY HAD...Research Buying Practices

-Quantify the Difference – (Show Improvement with Your Product/Service)

- ASK FOR THE ORDER

IT'S ABOUT TIME

Probably the most widely used clichés in our profession are centered on time and time management. *Timing is Everything; There is No Time Like the Present; Time is Money; Time is A Wastin';* and I bet you could name many more.

It has been my experience that Time Management is the single most important aspect of professional sales. I have also observed that some of the most professional business people have very little discipline when it comes to Time Management. This rings true all the way up the corporate ladder. Business people who have had no professional sales training are particularly egregious. In terms of self-motivation and self-improvement, the most significant course, seminar or training session I attended was a class on Time Management. It gave me a new perspective on the importance of scheduling events and sticking to that schedule.

One of the things that the course taught was that you should set your watch 15 minutes ahead and conduct your day accordingly. The obvious reaction to this instruction was, won't you know that your watch is set ahead and then what good will that do? As the instructor pointed out, and as I can attest after many years of employing this method, it makes you constantly aware of the time and your schedule. Now, I am not saying that I am never late, but only on very rare occasions.

Another thing that was pointed out in the course was that generally speaking, tardiness is an indication that you do not want to be where you are. Boy did that register home with me. I can remember being late consistently for a Monday morning Sales Meeting for no apparent reason. In reflection, I recall feeling that the meeting was a waste of time and the Branch Manager only held the meetings to hear herself talk. Yes, I was acting out.

As an extension of this self-analysis, I could hear my Mother's voice in my head saying, "People do what they want to."

What do you mean; people do what they want to? People do what they can. If people do what they want to, then I would be a millionaire—plain and simple, end of case. Only after my new awareness and for the first time did I hear and understand Mom's follow-up:

"No son. You don't want to be a millionaire. You wish you were a millionaire, and there's a big difference. What have you done to become a millionaire? Have you ever asked a millionaire how they became one or for instructions on how you might become one? Where's your plan for becoming a millionaire; and where are you in your plan?

It's hard to believe that a Time Management course took me down this road, but for me this was real clarity. My goodness, this course had conjured up some deep-rooted elements of my psyche. It took this training and nearly 40 years of living for me to understand what Moms was saying. The motivation for doing and not doing comes from within. All the times I made excuses for not completing my chores or not behaving in a certain prescribed manner, that indelible voice in my head, and my defiance to it...oh my.

I have also noticed that most of my good ideas were only good if I acted on them right away. The longer I waited to act on them, the less of a good idea they became. Even though it seems a bit impulsive, I have come to realize the importance of not waiting to commit to action. For me, the deliberate, well thought through, evaluation process has only added to my natural proclivity for procrastination—at which I tend to be real good. I am stating for the record that when it comes to the launching phase of a project or task, I admit I am a sinner. I can hem and haw with the best of them, but now I am fully aware of causes and ramifications of acting or not acting on a timely basis.

In summary, if you want to be on time, you will be. If you want to be successful, you will be. Define the terms, set the course and proceed.

THEY DON'T CALL THEM "COLD" FOR NOTHING

Because canvassing is a necessity to any sales effort and cold calling is a natural extension of canvassing, cold calls have to be made. Cold calls in the form of door knocking are a frightening endeavor. Early in my career I would hear senior Salespeople, almost in a chant, repeatedly say, "I love cold calling." For most of my career, it was my contention that they were liars.

That is, until I worked for the owner of a company who actually seemed to relish going out into the territory and knocking on doors. He was an extrovert who was a successful local businessman. What the heck? There was no fear of rejection in his mind. With him, *beating the bushes* took on a whole new meaning. He used the opportunity to laud his success. Secure in himself and buffered by his standing in the business world, the traditional worries and stresses did not come into play.

A bag carrying Sales Rep is not afforded such crutches. We have to take on and fight through each new encounter where the fear of rejection is a real factor. I tried reading about various techniques and even tried emulating successful Reps that I had a chance to work with out in the field, but that didn't make it any easier for me. Don't let anybody try to demean this phenomenon. It is a natural human emotion. Overcoming this innate fear occurs only with persistence and experience.

Fresh out of IBM Sales School and in my first territory, I found the cold calling aspects of the job so debilitating that I simply had to formulate a game plan to attack the problem. I decided to dedicate two hours per day to doing nothing but cold calls. I came up with this idea all on my own, and I thought it was brilliant. From the hours of 9:00 a.m. to 11:00 a.m. each day I would do nothing but cold call. Guess what? After almost a month, I realized that for those two hours each day I had set aside for cold calls, I did nothing. What I discovered was that the plan was without conviction. Mere drawing board rhetoric just won't do. You might say I sold myself a bill of goods. This strategy had set me on a course for ruin.

It was only after a company driven, new product, mail campaign was announced that I began to see the light. I submitted the company names and addresses from my territory into the Word Processing Center and the announcement of a hot new product was sent out. Management insisted that we make a personal visit to each company that was sent a letter. So, I stated in each letter that I would be "stopping by" in the next few days when I was in the area. Major emphasis was placed on this effort. This turned out to be a pivotal point in my selling career. Not every visit was a hit, but what seems so obvious now, and not so apparent then, was that the letter established a reason for my being there. This was a reason that helped me to get beyond the Gatekeepers. The letter was not sent to them, so how could they determine if my visit was valid, or not.

"I'm here in follow-up to a letter I sent Mr. Big. Would you let him know I'm here?" Because I had clearly stated in the letter that I would be stopping by, my visit could not be considered *unannounced.*

"Oh, didn't you get my letter? Do you have a moment to discuss it now or perhaps I could make an appointment? Now, this was no panacea, but I felt light years ahead of the game. I planned my cold calling around my mailings. I sent 25 pieces of mail each week and made five follow-up calls each day of the following week, between the hours of 9:00 a.m. and 11:00 a.m., until the process of knocking on doors became routine. I used a variety of themes in my letters ranging from new products to cost-saving analyses and every now and then I would even get a warm welcome and a thank you for the informative correspondence.

Yea, I can hear you pros out there saying, "Mail can't and won't do your selling." I suppose you're right, but for me this was a right of passage on the road to Damascus. With respect to cold calling, I had discovered the Rules of Engagement.

Having said all of that about my cold calling adventures, I must acknowledge that the norm for modern-day successful cold calling and canvassing has changed. Door knocking techniques are a bit more sophisticated today. Sales people are a very resilient and resourceful group by nature. Some changes were forced upon us for the sake of efficiency and some changes had to be made because of sheer logistics. Can you imagine the conventional approach to cold calling on the Federal Government in Washington, D.C.? Can you say SECURITY?

Successful professional Salespeople employ a mixture of trade shows, conferences, exhibits, seminars, Chamber of Commerce events, and promotional ad campaigns to attract customers and present their wares. These methods in conjunction with well thought out strategies for follow-up can be extremely effective and productive.

In fact, I say to this day that I still enjoy attending and presenting at Business Shows. That's right, you heard me, "I love manning the booth!" I have found that these events allow for two-way selling. Exhibitors can show-off their stuff and attendees (Salespeople in disguise) have a captured audience to whom they can make a pitch and gather information about the companies being represented. Often times the company's top executives will be in the booth briefly. It may very well be the only time you get to meet with that decision maker. On more than one occasion I have been told by a number of "important people" that they were too busy to meet with me no matter what I was selling, only to turn around and run into them at a local business convention where they were cornered and then somewhat obligated to listen to my spiel. ("Hi there! I'm the nice sales guy with a family to support, trying to earn a living by working hard to show people, like you, how my products and services can help your company be more profitable and cost efficient, thereby making your shareholders and every member of your organization more confident in your ability to deliver the goods. But of course, none of that is important to you because—you're too busy?") Without question, some of my most significant sales came from a lead or contact made at a Business Show or Conference.

Professional Associations and User Groups also seem to be fertile ground for establishing and nurturing good contacts and relationships. They provide for like-minded thoughts and attitudes. I guess it can be viewed as a fellowship of professional sales; a place for networking and attitudinal adjustment. A lot of Salespeople will tell you that local watering holes provide for much of the same.

MY POINT OF REFERENCE

As any Sales Rep will tell you, a customer reference can be a powerful tool in gaining the edge on your competition, and of course, the Golden Rule of using references is to be sure to confirm with the *reference* that it is okay to do so. You would be surprised to find out just how often Reps overlook the Golden Rule. Now, all of this probably seems so rudimentary, but references are a big deal and I have witnessed, on several occasions, in big deals and by some pretty Senior Reps, the results of not confirming a reference. In each case, there was the assumption that because there was a certain amount of rapport with the customer and because there was never a complaint, that all was well. We all know what happens when we...ASS U ME.

The prevailing wisdom among buyers and decision makers who are asked to sign on the dotted line (especially for the first time) is that—well, they are dealing with 'Salespeople', you know; they wouldn't put it past us...; buyer beware; and all that stuff. They want to know: where; with whom; how much; and to what degree your success can be measured. In fact, to Federal Government Buyers references are known as "Past Performance."

The following is my recollection of another career altering event about which I simply must share.

Sure enough, shortly after my return from Sales School, I was promoted to the position of Copier Specialist—a quasi-management role that provided sales and technical support to the Field Reps. Our Branch was in the middle of some heavy competition in a number of large, high profile accounts. After several weeks of demonstrations and proposal submissions at one particular account, I accompanied the Branch Rep to the Best and Final Offer (BAFO). We sat across from three procurement specialists who had been delegated to evaluate the competing products. Although our product seemed to successfully address all of the customer's applications, both the Rep and I were uneasy with the cascading vibes. (Experienced

Salespeople tend to develop a sixth sense about customer intentions when it comes to *closing time.*)

The lead specialist looked me in the eye and said, "Because this is quite a substantial purchase, we are looking at every aspect of the decision very closely. And, although we don't usually share one vendor's information with another, because we like your products, we thought you should be aware of a pretty persuasive bit of information that is serving as ammunition for us to select another vendor. It's a matter of one of the references."

What the heck does he mean 'references'? I had personally provided the references for our proposal. Five of them, in fact; three local and two national. What kind of cruel joke is this? Are we being *gas lighted*?

"I assure you that these are sincere references from some of our very satisfied customers," I told the specialist.

"Oh no, not your references. I am talking about your chief competitor's references," he responded. "Mrs. Jones checked and verified all of the vendor references and brought something very interesting to my attention. X Company provided your company as one their references. When we asked X Company if they were sure that they wanted to supply this reference, they not only assured us of the reference, but said it was okay to inform you of what they had done. Your company refused to give us a lot of information, but they did confirm that they were a large user and have been for quite some time. They also admitted that they had recently upgraded their large machines to the very ones that X Company is now proposing to us."

I could see it in my mind. Oh man, what a coup. This was the ultimate sales one-up-man-ship. The memo must have read:

TO: ALL PROSPECTIVE CLIENTS
FM: X COMPANY
RE: WHO'S THE BEST?

Our products are so good our competitors use them instead of their own products. They especially like them when considering cost and performance.

Demoralized by this experience, we limped back to the office. Although angry and frustrated, we could hardly say a word. I was disappointed in our company and the Rep was disappointed in me. I researched the referenced division of our company that was using "those" machines and fired off a letter to the General Manager. This engendered an initial response and several deteriorating responses back and forth. In the end, we simply had to agree to disagree. Corporate never budged and neither did I.

Class, do you have any thoughts on this one…?

As a salesman in the Office Products Div., I am appalled to think of our company using the competitors equipment. I am speaking specifically about some of our divisions that are using Xerox 9400 copiers. Don't we believe in our own products? Do you realize how our competitors use this fact against us? If we can't make a product to compete, then we should get out of the business. At the very least we should make every attempt to adapt our applications to fit our equipment. In no case should we be using the competitor's equipment.

I firmly believe that this matter should be investigated closely. There is no reason why we should give our competitors this kind of ammunition to stall our sales efforts. And - with the outrageous quotas given to the sales force this year, we don't need negative aspects in our program such as this.

Just imagine a prospective customer considering an IBM Series III, and a Xerox Copier and, the Xerox Company gives the IBM Corp. as a reference for their box. How do we compete in the face of this?

So mad I am numb,

Speak Up # 0158

(Illustration II)

International Business Machines Corporation

Office of the General Manager
Command and Space Systems
Federal Systems Division

18100 Frederick Pike, Gaithersburg, Maryland 20760

April 8, 1980

Dear IBMer,

Within the Gaithersburg facility we have two distinct reproduction requirements:

o   high volume reproduction, which is performed in the Technical Publications Reproduction department — last year they reproduced five million copies and this year we project an increase to over seven million.

o   convenience copying activity, which is performed on a self-service basis on 21 IBM Series II copiers throughout the facility.

In 1979, based on our high volume, quick turnaround requirements, and the inability of the Series III to perform when used in a high volume mode, we initiated a series of studies to determine what reproduction configuration was required for our reproduction operation. Studies revealed that each of the two Series III copiers in operation were producing 120,000 copies per month. This study, which covered the period between March 1977 (installation date) and May 1978, also revealed a daily volume of 10,840 copies and an average of from 15,047 to 18,569 copies between maintenance calls, due solely to our high volume copying.

In May 1978 OPD Field management recommended we add two Series III's to alleviate our down time problem. This recommendation of four units at the internal IBM rate was less costly than one competitive machine. However, operator labor for the four Series III's would have cost us more per copy than one Xerox 9400 with one operator.

In view of these facts, the decision was made to replace the two Series III copiers with one Xerox 9400. This decision was agreed upon by FSD executive management as well as OPD Headquarters and in August 1979, a Xerox 9400 was installed in a controlled area of our Technical Publications Reproduction department.

Thank you for bringing your concern to my attention. I can certainly understand your position and trust you will understand ours.

Sincerely,

Gerald

(Illustration III)

CLUBHOUSE RULES

My first year was a doozy, full of career altering experiences. Although our Marketing Managers did a good job of introducing and explaining the "comp" plan, I was never quite prepared for the almighty Chargeback. Chargebacks could totally nullify a good month or year.

CHARGEBACK (n): Not all equipment was sold on NET terms. The copiers and automated typewriters were also rented and leased. If the customer returned the equipment—even if the leasing period had ended—the Rep was "docked" the value of that piece of equipment. That was particularly crushing when you consider that the Rep who was forced to take the chargeback might not have been the Rep who sold the equipment. Just imagine sailing along at about 110% of Y-T-D quota attainment at the end of the third quarter, and then being notified (by way of a 30 day notice) that one of your customers was canceling several pieces of equipment, valued at about two months worth of quota, that you never sold.

The circumstance depicted above was not uncommon. It happened to a number of Reps, including yours truly. As devastating as the fourth quarter chargebacks were to my first year, it taught me an invaluable lesson—my first head-on experience with the importance of professionally managing the territory. Never again did I take for granted that the customers would renew the contracts. You can refer to it as "customer service", "customer care", hand-holding", or whatever you like, but getting and staying in touch with the customer proved to be an absolute must.

There was one other positive effect from the chargeback experience. I was doggedly determined not to let them effect my second year. Nothing could have stopped me from achieving quota in my second year. The "kid" was smokin'. I was one of the leaders in several categories not only in the Branch but in the Region, as well. Today, almost 30 years later, I still have some of the wall plaques and congratulatory letters I received as a result of that year. If memory serves me, I think I was in the 100% Club by September.

100% CLUB: A designation signifying 100% of the yearly quota assignment-OR-the thing you don't want to miss too many times. Even during the early days, 100% Clubs were ever pervasive. Most companies with large sales forces had some form of a 100% Club to recognize their successful Salespeople. I would almost be willing to bet you that nobody brainwashed their sales force like IBM about the grandiloquence of being a member of the 100% Club. Pardon my characterization.

"Well, you made it I see." I was not quite sure how to respond because I did not recognize the gentleman who uttered the phrase. "This must be your first."

"I am really glad to be here," I responded. Yes, this was my first 100% Club.

The rookies stood out like a sore thumb. The looks on our faces ranged from awestruck to lottery winner. Again and again, what must have been 100 people that I had never met before congratulated me. The more they congratulated me, the more trite my response became. Why was my ability to communicate so diminished? I was just like all the other starry-eyed rookies. However, some were pitiful—a real embarrassment. I remember one of the rookies from my office that actually walked around looking at people and things like he was in Heaven—pupils fully dilated mouth agape, limp posture, and clumsily moving about. I was just waiting for him to collapse in ecstasy.

January 26, 1978

Dear Ty,

Congratulations on qualifying for the 1977 One
Hundred Percent Club. 1977 was a mixed bag in a
lot of areas, but for the Bethesda Branch it was
a great year, and to that end I know that your
contributions were significant.

Ty, we're going to Los Angeles for the first time
and I can assure you from the previews I've seen
of the Club it's bigger and better than ever.
It will also afford people like yourself the
opportunity to renew many acquaintances you've
made over the years.

Again, congratulations and I look forward to
welcoming you personally in March.

Dick

Mr. T. L. Cypress
Marketing Representative
Bethesda Branch Office

(Illustration IV)

T. R. ▮▮▮▮▮
Person's Pond Drive, Franklin ▮▮▮▮▮▮ 87417

February 10, 1978

Dear Ty:

Congratulations on achieving your second Hundred
Percent Club.

In 1977 our business climate made attainment
particularly challenging and your success is a
compliment to your dedication and ability.

I personally appreciate your effort. You have my
best wishes for your continued success, and I look
forward to seeing you in Los Angeles.

Sincerely,

Mr. Tyrone Cypress
Bethesda 02B
Region 5

(Illustration V)

T. E.
400 Parson's Pond Drive, Franklin Lakes, New Jersey 07417

January 10, 1979

Dear Ty:

Congratulations on qualifying for your third Hundred Percent Club.

Qualification in the Club is never an easy achievement. However, 1978 particularly tested us and I recognize the effort and ability that were required to attain this important goal. You should take great pride in your success.

My best wishes for your continued success.

Sincerely,

Mr. T. L. Cypress
Bethesda OP #02B
Region 5

(Illustration VI)

J. V. ███████
Parson's Pond Drive, Franklin Lakes, New Jersey 07417

February 20, 1980

Dear Ty,

Congratulations on qualifying for your fourth Hundred Percent Club.

You accepted the demands of 1979 and performed well. You should take pride in your achievement. Individual performances like yours are the key to the success the Office Products Division has enjoyed.

Congratulations again. I look forward to seeing you in Miami.

Sincerely,

Jack

Mr. T. L. Cypress
Bethesda OP #02B

(Illustration VII)

J. V. ██████
Parson's Pond Drive, Franklin Lakes, New Jersey 07417

February 20, 1980

Dear Ty,

Congratulations on qualifying for your fourth
Hundred Percent Club.

You accepted the demands of 1979 and performed
well. You should take pride in your achievement.
Individual performances like yours are the key to
the success the Office Products Division has
enjoyed.

Congratulations again. I look forward to seeing
you in Miami.

Sincerely,

Jack

Mr. T. L. Cypress
Bethesda OP #02B

(Illustration VII)

E. L. ▐▇▇▇▇▇
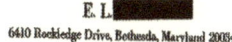
6410 Rockledge Drive, Bethesda, Maryland 20034

December 30, 1980

Dear Ty,

Congratulations on qualifying for the 1980 One Hundred Percent Club!

Being one of the pace setters in your office, it came as no surprise that in spite of the tough year that 1980 turned out to be, you still managed to beat the mark. I share with you in the excitement of an excellent performance.

Thank you again, and I look forward to seeing you in Los Angeles.

Sincerely,

Ed ▐▇▇▇▇▇▇

Mr. Tyrone L. Cypress
Account Representative
Washington Suburban

(Illustration IX)

J. R. ▓▓▓▓
400 Parson's Pond Drive, Franklin Lakes, New Jersey 07417

January 7, 1981

Dear Tyrone,

Congratulations on qualifying for your fifth Hundred
Percent Club.

Your achievement represents the pursuit of
excellence required in our competitive marketplace
and I appreciate your contribution.

Best wishes for your continued success, and I look
forward to seeing you in Los Angeles.

Sincerely,

Dick

Mr. T. L. Cypress
B/O #02B
Washington Suburban OP

(Illustration X)

February 12, 1981

Dear Mr. Cypress,

Congratulations on your fine sales performance and on
qualifying for your fifth Hundred Percent Club! This
is an important milestone, and I am grateful for the
contributions you are making to IBM.

You have my best wishes for continued success in the
future.

Sincerely,

Mr. T. L. Cypress
OP 02B
IBM Corporation
1550 Research Boulevard
Rockville, MD 20850

(Illustration XI)

HUSTLE: THE 'X' FACTOR

Am I a good salesman? I must admit I used to spend a lot of time on this question. How do you measure a Salesperson? Is it by how they rate in comparison to the Reps with whom they have worked? Is it the size of the deals or income, percentage of closes, or plaques on the wall? It's all so muddled.

Over the years I have concluded that it's not worth contemplating. The question is too situational and too circumstantial. There are too many variables.

At an award ceremony I saw a Rep receive top honors for achieving her annual quota objectives. She ranked in the top 1% of a very large sales force. Was she a good Sales Rep? How about the fact that she was about to marry a very high-ranking government official in the Agency where she made most of her sales? What about the Salesman who closed one of his company's largest sales to a school system where his Mother was on the Board? How about the companies awarded Government contracts without a bidding process?

In fact, some of the deals I have seen closed could very well be called *Acts of God*. Pass-throughs, shell games—how does an honest hardworking Sales Rep compete? I have come to grips with the fact that the world of professional Sales may not be fair, but it's my world just the same. Suck it up, full steam ahead, no excuses, eyes on the prize, charge 'til I fall, then do it all again!

HUSTLE—this is the "X Factor"! When I'm hustling, I'm selling. This is another one of those lessons that found its way into my psyche by way of professional happenstance.

I responded to a newspaper ad wherein there was an invitation to attend an open seminar/briefing session to hear all about this new line of products, needing some top-notch Salespeople. The ad said those looking for a new start or a career jump should be sure to attend.

As it turned out, the function was surprisingly well attended. A full parking lot and a room full of 'hopefuls'—a real mixed group. Ten percent were Xerox/IBM-looking—three piece suits—you know the type, stalled careers but too proud and polished to let go of the image; a large contingent of 'polyesters'; a splattering of sport coats and white shoes; and of course, a few genuine entrepreneurs looking for a ground floor opportunity.

Our host welcomed us and thanked us for our attendance and went on to assure us that we were in for something special. His presentation was complete with foils and flip charts. He started with the history of business in America (not really, but it seemed like it) and incorporated a timeline right up to and including the present. I can hardly remember anything he said beyond the beginning of his address where he used the all pervasive *triangle* to make several points. I couldn't help but think that there must be a rule that says when you gather two or more Salespeople in a room, you must draw a *triangle*.

After a good twenty minute business case, his presentation actually started to reach a crescendo (sort of). I'll give him credit; he had most of us on the edge of our seats in anticipation of this fantastic new product. He walked over to the table on the stage, stood behind it, and began to open the rather large box—large enough to hold a 26" television set. He reached in and pulled out a big, shiny, spanking-new...skillet. He then pulled out several matching pieces that served to complete the set. (A frying pan..? My goodness, had it all come to this? Can you imagine dressing up for this opportunity?) WHOA! The entire audience was numb.

It was obvious that the presenter was expecting some response from the crowd, but none was coming. There was just an uncomfortable silence. The presenter, sensing the impasse, displayed some remarkable composure. He positioned himself at the front of the stage and called for a short 15 minute intermission.

"Now," he said, "when we reconvene, I am going to ask that only those of you who are genuinely interested in pursuing this remarkable opportunity return. For those of you who have a sincere desire to get ahead in the business world, I'll share with you the merits and rewards of our program. And yes, for the record, we are going to talk about selling pots-and-pans."

He continued, "For those of you who choose not to return, please accept this as a chance to politely part company. I appreciate your attendance and attention today."

The crowd disbursed quickly and through it all, I spotted a familiar face across the room, and I'm sure he recognized me as well. We had worked for the same company. Good, I thought, I'll catch-up with him and get the benefit of his thoughts. As I tried to get closer, it became obvious that he was trying to avoid me. He kept looking away and moving with a purpose. He was embarrassed to be there. Even years later, when we ran into each other at a business show, he never did mention the "pots-n-pans" seminar.

Being the inquisitor that I am, I had to return for the follow-up session. From more than 100, only five returned. Interestingly enough, of the five who returned, I was the only one wearing a suit. Conspicuously absent were the young professionals, women and any semblance of diversity represented in the initial group. I was the lone "ethnic."

Our host was noticeably disappointed in the low number of returnees. He tried to put a successful spin on the deal—talking about the percentages and the likelihood of the number returning generating a better than average capture of canvassing ventures. Bulls*#$! If he was so pleased with the number of people who returned, why did his demeanor and tone rapidly deteriorate when talking about the folks that did not return? In fact, he became a lot less gracious in dismissing them, their motives, and their professional sincerity and commitment. Nevertheless, the presenter went on to explain the opportunity and the 'top side' rewards; however, I couldn't help but wonder how you would sell enough of these things to make any money?

Now comes the true separator. The host explained that in order to get started we would need to purchase a demo or starter kit for $250.00. The company would reimburse the Rep for that amount when he reached a certain number of sales. After a bit of back and forth and clarification, only one of the remaining Reps opted for the commitment and signed on to the program. I said, "Thanks, but no thanks."

A couple of weeks later, I ran into this Rep at the *'VENDevous'*.[1] I recognized him as soon as I pulled into the lot. He was busy loading his trunk with boxes that he was taking from the truck parked next to him. He and the gentleman helping him seemed to be having a good time as they chuckled while they worked. I parked just a few feet away and went over to say 'Hi.' I asked if he remembered me and how things were going.

"Oh, sure I remember you," he said. "Things are terrific. Someday, at happy-hour perhaps, I'll get a chance to tell you all about it, but for now I've gotta scat."

Now I didn't start out everyday at this location, but everyday that I did, I noticed this fellow was there loading his trunk or pulling out of the lot as I was pulling into the lot. He was the epitome of 'Beehive Selling.'

The one time that I did run into him at an evening sales gathering (happy-hour), he actually found and singled me out where he proceeded

---

1. A parking lot in a large industrial park near a Metroplex that was a great point of connection for area Reps to meet and hook-up for joint calls and an ideal place for merchandise Reps to pick-up, drop-off and exchange products. In the good ol' days it was safe to leave your car in an unsupervised parking lot and you didn't have to pay for parking.

to pepper me with questions about people (contacts) he could approach and use (reference) me as a conduit. He was gathering referrals and he was doing this with practically every person that would stop long enough to give him the time of day. He was workin' the room.

About six or seven months later, after a real long and hard day, I went to the regular happy-hour spot and noticed that the parking area was completely full. That meant that I had to go to the other side of the facility to find a parking space. This parking area was near an alternate entrance that allowed me to observe some of the functions going on in the ballrooms and meeting halls in the hotel where many companies held seminars and gathered to hand out awards and special recognition to their successful Reps.

As I walked down the hall, I noticed one of the meeting room doors open just enough for me to peek in and observe that the 'pots-n-pans' company was having an awards ceremony and that none other than "my guy" was sitting on the stage. Of course I had to stop and signify.

After a few minutes of eavesdropping I heard the presenter say, "…and now, it's time for our special award to our top Sales Rep in the Country."

It was you-know-who! Everyone in attendance rose to their feet and cheered as "my guy" got up to receive his award. As he stood there the presenter read off a list of some of his achievements. Well, well, I thought, hats off to my man. I couldn't help but think how hard this guy must have worked to garner this kind of success. I also thought about how so many of us had passed on this opportunity—quite frankly, because we thought it was beneath us.

Several weeks later I encountered him at the *VENDevous*. He was sitting in a large truck and there were two guys taking boxes out of the truck and putting them into their trunks. That was a sight that needed no further explanation. So what does all of this have to do with HUSTLE? I left

there convinced that he had "the 'X' factor" and that was the real discrimi-
nator.

SAL(E)ACIOUS

Sex sells—fact or fiction? My experience somewhat belies convention. I have found that appealing to that emotion may open a number of doors and promote a heightened level of enthusiasm, but it won't necessarily get the deal.

As the VP for a small computer company, responsible for management of the Sales Force, I was tasked with recruiting and hiring. In an attempt to expand the Sales Force, I placed an ad in the local newspaper and began reviewing the resumes as they arrived. The pickins were sort of slim so, I asked my assistant to contact all of the candidates and schedule the interviews. The process was routine. However, I can remember one of the interviews stood out quite dramatically.

The receptionist buzzed me on the intercom to let me know that my 10:00 a.m. interviewee had arrived and she was waiting in the lobby. There was something about the tone of her voice.

"Okay, tell her I'll be with her momentarily," I said.

While I was looking for a copy of her resume, one of the administrative staffers walked into my office and said, "You've got to be kidding."

"What do you mean?" I asked.

"Is that lady in the lobby here for an interview?"

"Why, yes," I said. "Is there a problem?"

The staffer turned and walked away but I could hear her say, "Well, let's just say she's a little bit different."

Just then the company President stuck his head in my door and said, "My man! Way to go! You've got my approval."

Now that was out of character, I thought. Besides, at this point, I was not sure what he was talking about. I finally found the resume and went to the lobby to meet her.

WOW! I'm glad I saw her before she saw me. I needed that moment to make sure I did not seem affected one way or another, but this lady was not just attractive, she was sexy—way outside of corporate acceptance. She had too much hair, too much make-up, and too much jewelry. Although her attire and appearance were not appropriate for professional sales, she was not vulgar. Nothing was too tight or too short.

I introduced myself and welcomed her to the company. She answered in a voice that I though was a put-on. Nobody talks like that, I thought to myself. She looked like Sophia Loren and sounded like Marilyn Monroe. Usually attractive ladies in the workplace don't faze me at all, especially after working at Exxon Office Systems where most of the sales ladies looked like models, but this lady…now it was clear what caused all the commotion.

From here I'll refer to her as Miss Kay. Normally I start the interview process by getting the candidate to talk about their experience and why they think they can make a difference on the job but as I reviewed Miss Kay's résumé, I noticed that she had no sales experience. I raised this issue and she explained that she was making a career change and was willing to start at the beginning and earn her stripes. She had done a lot of reading and was fascinated by the sales process. It was at that point I had to bring up the matter of her appearance. I went into a long diatribe about fitting in and being appropriate. After my sermon, convinced that I had just changed her mind (and a little worried that I might have hurt her feelings) I could see that she was unwavering in her decision to become a Sales Rep. I presented her with a number of challenging questions. We went back and forth for nearly 45 minutes.

Finally, I asked, "Are you willing and able to make the changes I suggested?"

She eagerly replied, "Will you teach me?"

I was simply floored by her enthusiasm and willingness to become a professional Sales Rep. And here's a confession that I never shared with her or anyone else: While interviewing her, I could not help comparing her to 'yours truly' in my initial interview at IBM—not as sexy but just as out of place.

Since I rarely extend an offer in the first interview, I told her that I would be in touch. Two days later, I offered her the job. When I announced at our staff meeting that I had made Miss Kay the offer, and she had accepted, two ladies on the staff resigned. They took umbrage with what they thought was a blatant disregard for professional ethics. So what, I thought, we are better off without them—even though one of them returned after only two months. Besides who knew best—them or me? I was convinced that Miss Kay was a natural with loads of potential so I stood by my guns.

With a real *let's go get 'em* attitude and a double dose of enthusiasm, Miss Kay started out with a bang. Unfortunately, there was a two-tiered learning curve she had to overcome. Not only did she have to learn sales, she had to learn our computer products and services, as well.

I thought that voice would be a knockout over the telephone for getting appointments and generating interest. Even the toned-down version of Miss Kay should have given new meaning to Customer Relationship Management. Sure enough, she got lots of appointments; however, just like a case of arrested development, there was no magic beyond that phase of the sell cycle. She had to work just as hard as the other Reps to get the business. In fact, even harder in some cases.

I remember confiding with one of my more senior Reps at how surprised I was that the business did not come a little easier for Miss Kay. The Rep seemed equally surprised at my pronouncement.

"Tyrone, you really didn't think it would be any easier for her, did you? Just imagine, once she managed to get beyond all the folks that resented her for her looks, who immediately classified her as a 'type' and not as a professional business woman, she had to deal with the decision makers who were only reminded of the girl who was unreachable and turned them down when they asked for a prom date. Remember, it's like you always tell us, this is high-tech stuff we are selling. We are trying to get our customers to make business decisions not emotional decisions."

I slowly surfaced from her echoed eloquence—a dose of reality.

Unlike the Hollywood version of this story, Miss Kay was not my top producer, but she was my hardest worker. She represented proof of how persistence and dedication can pay off. Today Miss Kay and her husband operate their own business and are still dear friends.

BEATITUDENTAL

<u>ODE TO A SALES REP</u>

Blessed are those who sell
  door to door;
Sell used cars or telemarket;
And especially those who sell
  to the Federal Government -
The world's hardest customer
  to satisfy!

For they are a hard working
 and dedicated group
Who do it to earn a living
But are often times maligned,
 misunderstood, and in need
 of ...

- A HUG -

BEEF SPEW

In selling to the Federal Government, a lot of the decision makers and influencers are Chief Information Officers and Information Technology Strategists. Ideally they represent the collective group to whom we as 'sellers' try to contact and present our wares. However, they are almost impossible to corner long enough to get the chance. They seem to go from seminar to seminar pontificating and espousing their philosophies about how the IT world should operate. The thing that gets me is how they will show up at these functions, be a member of a panel discussion, talk in detail about the past, present, and future of the computer world—but forget to bring a business card. The real reason is that they simply don't want to give out their contact information. They don't want to be engaged by Salespeople.

I recall a meeting wherein the Chief Information Officer of a large federal agency stood before the audience and bragged about her agency's commitment to do business with minority firms and how they were planning to exceed their Spend Goals. This presentation was actually being broadcast on closed circuit television and there was a 'real Congressman' on the panel. She went on and on about how accessible she was and encouraged the vendors in the audience to be in touch with her to present any and all products and services that might help their Information Technology efforts.

What a crock! She had no intentions of talking to any vendors. Her phone and e-mail access were so screened it was incredible. Her screeners weren't just evaluating products and services, they were sifting out WHO not WHAT! In a meeting with one of the agency's screeners, I was told in a pointed manner that one of the managers had over 1,800 unopened e-mails. These were the managers whose responsibility it was to evaluate vendor offerings—when was this person going to open the e-mails? How come there were so many? I submit that this was not a case of being overwhelmed with requests for opportunities to do business; it was a matter of being under whelmed with the conviction and commitment to do the job they were hired to do.

Don't tell me "I'm too busy..." Nonsense—answer the phone, answer your e-mails! I'll guarantee the folks who don't have time for Salespeople were never in a sales position. I say that not because of the lack of respect that they show Salespeople, but any professional who has had the training of a professional Salesperson would have developed the time management skills necessary to multitask and handle day-to-day routines more efficiently.

Too busy? I am not hearing that! If they are too busy to do the job, then give a portion of the work to someone else to help get the job done, OR give it all to someone who can do the job!

PERSONNALS

Here's another one for you.

While seeking a government contract, I had the occasion to attend a vendor's conference. This was an event where the agency requesting bids and pricing proposals sponsored a meeting to directly explain to the vendors what they were looking for and to answer questions in detail.

We all gathered in a medium sized auditorium. There were about 50 vendors present. I arrived early and was able to get a good seat in the front row. That was important because this allowed me the ability to make eye contact with the speaker at the podium. That is, it would have allowed me to make contact if she had bothered to look at me.

Its 9:00 a.m., time to begin. The Program Coordinator entered the room, walked across the stage and took her place behind the dais.

"Good morning, my name is Ms. O'Lady[1] and I will be acting as the Contracting Officer for this effort."

It was apparent to me that this lady had attended somebody's public speaking course. Her poise, posture, pronunciation and projection were impeccable. She took a deep breath, smiled, centered her papers and scanned the audience before beginning her presentation.

"As you may know, our Agency encourages new vendor participation, and I would just like to get some sense of the new vendors here today. So, would one representative from each new vendor stand and briefly introduce yourself?"

The last new vendor to stand (and he made sure he was last) and introduce himself was seated two seats from me. He stood and introduced him-

---

1.   Names have been changed to protect the innocent.

self as Mr. O'Gent.[2] He also said he was new to the area and single. From my vantage point, I could observe that from that moment until the vendor conference adjourned, the eye contact between Ms. O'Lady and Mr. O'Gent was never broken. It was as though they were the only two in the room.

At the end of the meeting, Ms. O'Lady asked if everyone had a copy of the new organizational chart. Of course we did, the chart wasn't so new; it was at least a month old, but of course, right on cue, Mr. O'Gent raised his hand to announce that he didn't have a copy. As the world turns, Ms. O'Lady invited Mr. O'Gent to accompany her back to her office where she would make a copy available to him.

Folks, this is where I jump off. Suffice it to say that I later found out that Mr. O'Gent had convinced Ms. O'Lady that his company could be a good supplier to her agency.

I'll leave this one open for the reader's interpretations and conclusions. Reflect on this situation as a case study offered for thought provocation. To divulge my innermost thoughts aloud would derail my objective and run the risk of offending. *You gotta' know when to hold 'em...know when to fold 'em...* Do you see any obvious business lessons in the pursuit of summoning up the 'natural' qualities necessary for development?

---

2.   Names have also been changed to protect the guilty.

GOT LUCK?

I can remember one year when our office was struggling to make quota as we rapidly approached the end of the third quarter. Each Rep was asked to make a full-blown presentation to the Branch Manager where he or she had to highlight their year-to-date activity and give a detailed forecast for the last three months of the year, showing how and when annual quota goals would be achieved, in the form of a flip chart presentation (something considered to be a big deal at the time). The Branch Manager, four Marketing Managers, and two Product Specialists were in attendance to monitor and evaluate every word. Although I was somewhat nervous about this review because of all of the Managers present, I was pretty much on target to-date so I anticipated I would get through the whole thing relatively unscathed.

As I got down to the business at hand, I was careful to point out how my performance had been consistent and I covered all the products to indicate that I had a command of the entire product line. This was crucial at IBM because recognition and promotions were tied into being able to sell all the products (especially dictation equipment). The presentation was going smoothly. In fact, too smoothly. Not one Manager bothered to ask a single question or bothered to challenge any of my numbers or any elements of my plan. I could not help but notice that the Branch Manager had actually fallen asleep. Just when I thought I was doing such a great job and making an impression on the Managers, it became obvious that they hardly heard a word I said.

It wasn't until I got to my 4th Quarter Forecast that any of them seemed to stir and show signs of life. On my final chart I not only forecasted quota attainment that qualified me for the 100% Club, but I called the number of units and the day that I would achieve quota. That got 'em! The sleeping Branch Manager sat straight up in his chair. He could not have been more awake once he saw my pronouncement. He got up and walked to the easel and tore off my forecasted number and the date I said it would happen.

He looked at me and said, "Good job."

He then left the Conference Room. One of the Product Specialists could not resist pointing out that on my first chart I had spelled the word forecast—f-o-r-c-a-s-t. Other than that little retort there were no comments.

Later that afternoon when I went into the Branch Manager's office, I noticed that behind his desk he had tacked the torn piece of paper from my chart onto his wall. That Forecast was now a Commitment.

In the following weeks things were relatively normal and went pretty much according to plan. But you know, sometimes the stars and planets line up just right. An order that I had been anticipating for nearly eight months finally closed. I went by the customer's office and picked up the Purchase Order two days before the date of my impending projection and *sandbagged* it for maximum effect.

On D-Day I walked into the Branch Manager's office and announced that I had just entered an order that satisfied my annual quota—bringing my Year-To-Date performance almost to the precise number of units that I had projected. The Branch Manager was beside himself. He leapt from his chair and congratulated me. He called one of the Marketing Managers into his office and told him the news and then he went out into the Sales area and made the office aware of what had taken place. At the next Sales Meeting, he made a really big deal of the situation by holding up the piece of torn paper from my flip chart and recounted the event for the entire Sales Force.

7 7 7

Speaking of being lucky…I am reminded of another time in a sales situation far removed from the previously mentioned encounter. I was the Educational Sales Rep for a large book company. I handled a geographic territory that covered the East Coast from Maryland through New England. One day I was informed by my immediate Manager that our corporate VP was going to be in my territory and had requested that I plan a full day of joint calls. I must admit, I was somewhat apprehensive about the short notice given to prepare for the VP's visit, but without too much work I prepared a full day's worth of calls and activities. As it turned out, it was a special day. Special not because of how much was sold, but because it was one of those days where I could seem to do no wrong.

We arrived at our first appointment. We were ten minutes early. I quickly turned to my Daytimer™ notes and shared what my goals were for the call. I told the VP that this was a follow-up call to ask the Decision Maker for an order. Until now, I had only been able to present my proposal to Influencers. We went in and the Decision Maker was sitting at his desk with a copy of my proposal right in front of him. I thanked him for seeing us and made the introductions.

Before I could transition to the next order of business, the Decision Maker said, "This is a great proposal! I can see why my folks are so impressed. I have already instructed them to prepare the Purchase Order for the titles and dollar amounts you have recommended. When do you think we can expect delivery?"

Since I had only recommended the titles we had for immediate delivery, I replied, "Within one business week."

I thanked him for the order and wrapped-up in the most professional manner I could muster. It was difficult to keep the juvenile adulation from spilling right out of me. The Decision Maker instructed me to coordinate the order processing and delivery with one of his staffers. As we headed for the Procurement Office, I stopped by the office of the lady who had been the most helpful in securing this order. I introduced her to the VP and thanked her for her assistance. Without provocation, she began to tell the VP how pleased everyone was with our products and services and especially with ME. She went on to say that I had a natural proclivity for customer service. Sure, this was one of my favorite accounts, but this morning's events surprised even me. Grateful for her comments, I thanked her again and we left.

At the end of the hall, I spotted the new Audio-Visual Director. He was standing in front of an office doorway talking to someone inside. I mentioned to the VP that I was trying to get an appointment with the AV Director to introduce him to our new line of CD-ROMs as I was convinced that it was the up and coming way of the futuristic classroom.

As we got closer to the AV Director, the VP said, "My goodness. He looks like an old friend of mine." (Naw...no way.)

Only a couple of paces away, I said, "Good morning."

The AV Director turned and returned the greeting. I could see as the VP and the AV Director made eye contact that they recognized each other. (Naw...no way?) For the next twenty minutes, or so, they went back and forth apologizing for not keeping in touch. It appeared they had been rather close at one time. They were from the same hometown, went to the same grade school and high school, and were in college together.

Finally, the AV Director asked the VP, "Well, what brings you here?"

The VP explained that he was traveling with one of his Reps (me) and to get a sense of how things were in the field.

"I've heard nothing but good things about this fellow (me)," said the AV Director.

"I know I owe you a return phone call, but I've been terribly busy trying to get established here," he told me.

"Well consider Tyrone an extension of your staff," offered the VP. "Feel free to call on him. He is very effective in supporting his clients." (Naw…no way!)

The VP then suggested, "Let's set you up as a test site for our new line of CD-ROM products? We'll provide a select group of users with the CD-ROMs and monitor their use and satisfaction with the products and, of course, these will be free trials. (This was significant because I would have had to get written approval from Corporate to offer a free trial of this size.) We'll only charge you for subsequent shipments once you are completely satisfied with the trial units."

"Why that's terrific!" exclaimed the AV Director. "I'll have a list of users to you by the end of the week."

He did just as he had said he would and the trials led to several significant orders over the next few months. As a matter of fact, this organization standardized on our CD-ROM products.

We were approaching the lunch hour, so the VP and AV Director insisted that we have lunch together. I reminded the VP of our intended destination—the Procurement Office. The VP suggested that I take care of the paperwork chores at the Procurement Office and then he and the AV Director would meet me at the Cafeteria. That's fine with me, I thought to myself. So far this is about as good as it gets for a Field Rep.

I completed my work at the Procurement Office and headed for the Cafeteria. When I got there I noticed that the VP and AV Director had not yet arrived. I took this time to check-in for messages. My first voice-mail message was from the adjoining area school district informing me of their decision to go with my proposal. They suggested I be in touch to schedule a time to review the terms and conditions and to finalize the order. Be in touch? Guess where we were going right after lunch? It was a slight departure from my planned day but imagine how the points were mounting now with my VP...

Lunch began to be a social endeavor as the VP and AV Director seemed to go on and on with their reunion. Anxious to get to the next account, I diplomatically wrapped up the now two hour lunch and we departed. On the way I explained to the VP that there was a good chance to secure another sizeable order, TODAY!

We entered the Administration Building of the second account and within minutes we found ourselves perched at the negotiating table. It became obvious that there was still some work to be done in completing the order but that was okay with me. I was prepared to stay as long as needed to get this order tied down. Nobody was getting up from this table until the deal was done. Ironically enough, it was the VP who caused the prolonged session. At practically every Contract Line Item Number (CLIN) the VP proposed larger quantities and authorized larger discounts. You could see that he was in his element. No wonder this guy had risen to the level of Corporate VP so quickly. By the end of the meeting, we had booked a very substantial order.

Unfortunately, we had come to quitting time. The VP thanked me for a most enjoyable day and commented that he was never more impressed with a Field Rep.

I think days like this one are often referred to as *being in the Zone*—when everything seems to fall into place. Although there have been times when I have closed major deals and had some good fortune in making my numbers and achieving my goals, I can't help but reflect on the specialness of that day.

Now, don't confuse me with Pollyanna. I know not everyday, not even most days, will turn out like this. And, there are probably a lot of Salespeople who might not think that this day was all that, but as you can see...don't take much to please me.

DOWN BUT NOT OUT

As a long time advocate for the profession, I guess I run the risk of painting a rosy picture about Sales and all that is required to be successful. For the record—Sales is a very demanding undertaking, and make no mistake about it, if you want to remain in the Sales profession, you must sustain a certain level of success. You must go out and bring home the bacon—or fish—or collards. I can hardly begin to relate some of the pitfalls, hurdles, and hard knocks that I have encountered along the way.

Of all the pressures and pains I have experienced, I must admit there's nothing quite like being fired. Now, I am not talking about being RIFed or let go because of downsizing or restructuring, that's different (although still painful). What I am talking about is being called into the office and being told that your services are no longer needed nor wanted. This is devastating to the professional ego as anyone who has ever gone through it will attest. Oh, and if you stay in the profession long enough, you will…

For more than 20 years it never happened to me. I never really worried about it. I always stayed one step ahead of the hatchet man. If things were not working out, I would simply move on down the road. Besides, the way I braced myself for that eventuality was to work hard each day and be prepared to blame my lack of success on any number of extenuating factors: bad economy; bad bosses; bad products; bad pricing; stiff competition; bad organization; etc. Sound familiar? We have all been there to one degree or another. If I failed, it just wasn't my fault, so I really didn't care if they fired me or not. In retrospect, what's funny is that all my armor only served as a good shield to defer the initial impact.

I remember being released from a Sales Management position at the end of a long, hard day, by two of the company principals. They called me in and explained that because their product sales were suffering they were forced to take the company into another direction—a direction that didn't include me. For months I had battled with the owners about one thing or another, so this didn't come as a complete surprise.

"Okay gentlemen, good luck to you in the future," was all I said.

In fact, I was visibly unshaken and did not give them the pleasure of seeing me fall apart—like so many of the other employees they had let go. Inside, it was yet another frozen moment in time.

Just look at 'em. Two dullards. One an old geezer and one a young buck—one 20 years over the hill and the other 20 years away from reaching his prime, and that's assuming he ever would. What audacity! How could they think for a moment that they could drive the sales of this company without me?

Oh how the wicked thoughts raced through my mind...

Well let's just see you move some of this dreck you call product without me. Who's going to find, hire and manage the new Reps? Who's going to tolerate the mismanagement of this dysfunctional, incompetent family run business and all of the misguided, uninformed business decisions? You know, I never really liked them anyway. Why was I so nice to them? I should have pointed out their faults and flaws a long time ago. How dare they try and make me the scapegoat while they were driving the business into the ground! It wasn't my idea to embrace that substandard, over-priced, thin margined, under functioned, awful suite of off-the-shelf products. Damn near impossible to sell and almost as hard to keep running. Service...what service? Our pitiful, way too many, untrained, inexperienced maintenance crew couldn't fix'o'dent. Hey! What about repeat business? What about renewals? Can you say 'customer service'? What about all of my recommendations for customer care and follow-up? Why didn't you ever do any of those things, huh? Why you ungrateful...

WHOA! Garçon, reality check please. These were two fine gentlemen who certainly didn't deserve to be the targets of my delirious venting. They had made a very calculated and understandable decision. The company was in trouble and letting me go steered the blame for its lack of success away from them. (Sound familiar?) From that perspective, how could

I be upset with their decision? They gave me an ample severance package and provided me with a chauffeured limousine ride home, after they took back the keys to the company car.

As fate would have it, I left that company and went on to one of the best jobs of my career and the manager who replaced me failed miserably and the company went out of business in less than two years…and justice for all.

INNER-VIEWS

I can't close out this segment of my career without mentioning the time between being fired from one position and being hired into the next, because therein lies the 'valley of the shadow of' for professional Salespeople—THE ABYSS! How do you maintain your integrity and your honesty and look into the eyes of an interviewer and say, "I was fired." After all, companies only want Salespeople who are or have been successful. If you were so good, why were you "fired"?

This poses a multifaceted dilemma. You must be honest and forthcoming and avoid the temptation to criticize your old employer and employees. (If I haven't mentioned it yet, this is a big **'no-no'** in an interview.) Oh, what to do? I struggled and stumbled through several interviews during this stretch of time. These were uncharted waters for me and I just couldn't close the deal.

My qualifications and experience were good enough to land me an interview with a large telecommunications company as the regional Manager heading up more than 200 Salespeople. The company actually outsourced the interviewing function to a consultant. He described the duties and requirements of the position and added that the base salary was over $250,000.00. I, of course, managed to make this the worst interview of my life. Although I felt that I could have done a masterful job in this position, I couldn't make the transition. While groping for the words to bridge me from that one failure to how and why I was the right person for this job, I could feel that I was coming across as a pretender. The interviewer was a real gentleman and he let me down easy. He promised to keep my resume on file and be in touch if the company executives wanted to talk further. I left knowing that he would never call and he never did.

Then there was the local newspaper that was expanding their business model to include a number of Internet services and required an entire sales force to do so. I interviewed for a position as one of the three Sales Managers they were hiring. After several interviews, I finally got the hiring manager to reveal how things really stood. Her comment to me was that of the top five candidates, I was in the top four. Keeping in mind that there were only three available positions, I guess that pretty much summed up how well I had impressed her.

I always thought that was a very mean thing to say; very ungracious. Needless to say, I didn't get an offer there either. Maybe that's why I was so glad that the sales of Internet services for that newspaper never got off the ground and failed miserably. (Hey gang, I'm only human.)

Another interview calamity occurred when I applied for a sales position with a large telephone appliance company. I guess by then the sense of desperation must have been apparent. I did a brief phone interview with the Branch Sales Manager and she asked me to come in for an interview. I arrived 15 minutes early and was asked to fill out a job application. I completed the application and after another 30 minutes had passed, a Secretary came out and informed me that the Branch Sales Manager was out of the office having her picture taken for an ad campaign and that she had asked that I interview with her assistant. I was led into the conference room where more time passed before the assistant arrived. She came into the room, sat down and began asking me the silliest, most inane questions you could imagine. Not only was I stood-up, but my future employment had just been put in the hands of a 19-year-old admin clerk. (Oh Lord, have I not reached the bottom?)

Two weeks later I received a letter from the assistant informing me that my application had been reviewed and it had been determined that I was not qualified for the position. Not qualified? Now this must be the bottom. After 20 years of sales and sales management I was being told by the admin clerk that I was not qualified to sell a line of telephone appliances...HAM MERCY! Where do I go from here? My black cloud was hanging so low I could reach up and touch it.

Finally, the clouds broke and the sun shone through. I ran across a small engineering firm that was run by an engineer with no sales background. He admitted he had no sales background. This is a true anomaly in the business world; a dream come true, a boss that admits to having no idea about how to sell. Of course, the company wasn't doing all that well and he was somewhat desperate.

The short version is that for the next four years, we knocked 'em dead. We tripled the revenues and the profits. In a little more than three years, we went from 37 base clients to over 200!

Ahhh, much better. Now the head is up and the swagger is back and above all, I was never dishonest and my integrity was left relatively in check. Was I good...or was I lucky? Call me lucky—I'll take it!

SAY IT LOUD...BUT IN TWO PAGES OR LESS

Writing an effective résumé is an art form. I should know, I have written plenty. Unfortunately, when your résumé reflects a lot of jobs, it's not always received as a positive.

I have learned what I consider to be the best way to point out a lot of experience in an honest format that makes the best impression. I attach a cover letter to each resume explicitly stating that the résumé is an effort to highlight my experience and qualifications. If every job is not reflected, there is no dishonesty in the absence of some of the jobs. [*Attached is a compilation of the positive elements of my career.*] The other aspects may be discussed in the interview. This approach has helped to minimize the screening that goes on in the HR offices where someone actually weeds out the resumes listing more than four or five positions. The importance of a well-crafted resume was made abundantly clear to me soon after I left IBM.

The job that lured me away from Blue turned out to be a catastrophe. Although I learned a lot, and managed to bolster my professional credits while doing well financially, the glory was short-lived and so was my tenure with the company. After about 18 months it was back to the streets. I had heard that Memorex was hiring Federal Sales Reps and remembered an associate telling me that Memorex had a major sole source contract for their heavy iron products (tape and disk storage devices). Hey, that's for me! I love those sole source contracts—avoid the bidding process altogether. I contacted the Federal Sales Manager and was able to impress him with my sales background and training. However, I was told that it would be six to nine months before there would be an open billet to bring me on board. This posed a slight dilemma. By this time, I was convinced that Memorex was the place for me but I could not be without gainful employment for those six to nine months. I decided to take an interim position with another company and hope for a speedy resolve at Memorex.

It came to my attention that a former co-worker had recently become a Manager with a large government integrator and was looking for Sales Reps. I called her, we talked for a while, and she asked me to send her my resume.

"It's just a formality. As soon as I get it I'll have my Branch Manager set up an interview, and we'll get you in here," she assured me.

A couple of weeks went by and I heard nothing. I inquired several times but to no avail. Another week went by and finally I got a note in the mail:

Dear Tyrone,

This is the worst damn resume I have ever seen! If I didn't know you I certainly wouldn't have recognized you from this résumé. A four and one-half page resume? You've got to be kidding, right? Call me. Let's talk!

Was it really that bad? When we met in her office, I could hardly wait to confront her in person.

"Well, what's so bad?" I asked. No 'how ya beens' or 'what's been happenins', I went straight for an explanation.

"First of all, Tyrone, you never send a resume more than two pages long. I've seen Vitaes and biographies shorter than your resume. And, what is this crap about you performing in the Navy Blue Jackets Choir and the Howard University Choir? Okay, you're a talented fellow, but all of that is irrelevant to the matter at hand."

Now you've done it, I thought to myself. Too long? Could it just be that she's jealous because I have more accomplishments than she does? There's lots of stuff worth mentioning, you know? Irrelevant? Do you know how hard it was for a non-Fine Arts student to get into the Concert

Choir at Howard University and perform a solo, I might add? It's a good thing you're not a man or I'd punch you in the mouth.

"Also, look here, Tyrone," she continued. "The fact that you played Command-League Softball is really not necessary. I'm looking for professional experience, not hobbies or pastimes."

Thinking to myself again—WOW! She just leapt from critiquing my resume to an all out castigation. Is no one interested in an all-around kind of guy?

"Nowhere is there any quantification by objective," she persisted. "How did you help these companies? Did you help them to make money and if so, how much? What impact, if any, did you have on their operation? How do you anticipate helping us? What is it in your background that would substantiate any such claims? Where's your cover letter?"

Now wait just a doggone minute, I thought to myself. Is this the same person that I worked along side of at IBM? Didn't I out perform her? In fact, wasn't she let go? I knew we were in a corporate office downtown, but it sure seemed like the woodshed to me.

After some major introspection, I decided that maybe there was something to what she said. Spawned by this severe undressing, I took it upon myself to look into the "professional" way to write a resume. I resubmitted my new resume and was hired one month later. I have done some serious research and had ample opportunities to submit more resumes and as a result, I have managed to develop quite a technique. Good lessons can be hard.

JUST 'TWEEN US SALES FOLKS

One of the things that I have truly loved about my stint in the sales profession is listening to the war stories of my Sales Brethren. These stories are always rich, colorful, credible, unbelievable, inspiring, and unending. Two or more Salespeople prompted by the mentioning of any event, occurrence, or encounter could serve as the starting point for many hours of war story exchanges; especially from the old-timers (10 years or more of experience). I used to relish in getting something started, whether at the local watering hole or leaning across the adjoining cubicles—while we should have been making telephone calls. All I had to do was relay a brief customer interaction or any bit of sales philosophy and the stories would begin to flow. Salespeople seem to have a natural inclination to *do you one better* or *get one up on you*. These sessions not only have redeeming entertainment value, but often times would result in some very profound statements surfacing. To the non-Salesperson I know this sounds like the realm of the B.S. artist, but I don't care. I love the war stories! I like the chatter and the camaraderie and the environment that they create. I submit, the best motivational tapes I have heard and inspirational books I have read could easily be classified as "war stories." Over the years, I have found that the following encapsulations have always served as good stimuli for some thought provoking interludes...just 'tween us Sales Folks.

THEATER OF THE ABSURD

At one time, the most difficult product to sell in my bag was the IBM Magnetic Card Typewriter. It had a $12,000.00 price tag and a relatively long sell cycle. Plus, it was during the time when office automation was not highly revered; however, there was a healthy commission associated with the sale, and it went a long way in helping to achieve quota. When I made my first sale I was elated. I had convinced the customer that there was a tremendous payoff in increased productivity with this sophisticated piece of equipment. We would come out and install, and train, and make sure all was right. The equipment configuration was comprised of an electronic typewriter that sat on the desk, a box component that housed the system smarts that sat next to the operator, and a small punch card sized plastic magnetic card that was inserted into the box component to serve as the medium for keystroke capture and production. I explained to the Secretary that each magnetic card had a capacity of 5,000 characters (50 lines, 100 charters each). She seemed impressed. The order was booked. Delivery was scheduled and since our Customer Service Representatives had the actual responsibility for training the user, I was sitting pretty.

I should have known that it could not be that easy. While leaning back in an almost chaise lounge position at my desk, counting my commission dollars and having visions of Rep of the Month ceremonies starring ME, I got a phone call from the Secretary. She was frantic. For some reason the Customer Service Rep was delayed in arriving for the scheduled training so the Secretary had started trying to use the machine on her own without directions.

"Mr. Cypress, I can't tell you how disappointed I am in your misrepresentation of this product. You assured us that each mag card had a 5,000 character capacity." Then she slammed down the phone.

I immediately raced to the customer site. The Secretary met me at the entrance down the hall from her office. Not only was she disappointed, I could see she was very angry.

"Now, Mr. Cypress, I know what you said, but there is no way that these mag cards can hold 5,000 characters!" she exclaimed.

"Of course they can," I said. "Let's take a look."

We proceeded to her office; she was three paces ahead of me and moving swiftly. By the time I got through the doorway she was already standing next to the typewriter.

"There," she said pointing at the typewriter. "Show me how you can get 5,000 characters on that mag card."

I didn't know what to say or do. I could not believe my eyes. Was this a joke? Maybe I was the target of a prank. I looked at the typewriter, I looked at her, and back at the typewriter. She looked only at me. We stared at each other in silence for about 15 to 20 seconds, neither of us knowing what to say. She was waiting for an explanation and I was waiting for a punch line. The Secretary had actually managed to roll the mag card into the typewriter platen and was attempting to type directly onto it. She thought you typed on the mag card and then placed it into the box compartment to perform the revision and word processing functions. Can you say 'disconnect'? What was she thinking? What was *I* thinking?

I'll spare you the subsequent back and forth that took place to resolve this situation because it's almost irrelevant to the plot of this saga. Although I was somewhat reluctant to share this story with anyone, I had to tell my Customer Service Rep. Of course, she had to tell management and they had to tell the Sales Force who saw fit to remind me of it for months afterwards. I am not sure if they are still laughing at me or not. This encounter was very instrumental in the formulation of my style and approach to future sales situations. For me, the most important points in this story were the lessons I learned: Importance of Conceptual Selling;

Importance of a Live Demonstration; Importance of Checklist Thoroughness; and I'm sure there are more.

WHAT'S THAT SMELL

One morning around 9:00 a.m., I went into the snack room where a table full of Customer Engineers were having coffee (as usual) and a rather animated conversation. It seemed as though one of them had a very unpleasant encounter with a customer. The coffee pot was empty (as usual) so as I stood there making a fresh pot, I couldn't help but hear what was being said.

"Can you believe that lady? I'm really thinking about suing!" said the CE "How could Joe (the CE Manager) be so insensitive to my feelings?"

After a few more choice railings, he stormed out of the room worked up into a real lather. I looked at the guys sitting at the table and said, "Now, you've gotta tell me what that was all about."

As it turned out, we had a customer who ran a business out of her home. Whenever her office equipment needed servicing the service technician would be dispatched to her home to affect the repairs. Here's the catch: the lady had an acute sensitivity to aromas of any kind, from aftershave, cologne or soap. This situation was so serious that the lady would call in for service directly to the service manager to confirm that her circumstance was understood and that the person coming out to perform the service was informed that they could not wear any products with a scent. In fact, she insisted that the Customer Engineer not bathe the day of the service call before coming to her home. She warned that if these conditions were not met she would sue the company for endangering her health.

More than once, our Service Manager had adhered to her demands. On one occasion, we actually had to send two different service people to perform service on her equipment. The first technician went out and was rejected at the door. When he arrived, the lady said she could detect a scent that made her dizzy. Sure enough, the technician did not have on any cologne or shaving products, but he did shower that morning before the call. The lady was outraged. She called the office and threatened to sue the Company, the Manager, and the technician. She made such a "stink" that the Manager guaranteed that another technician would be dispatched the next day and he would make sure that the technician would be unshaven, unbathed, and free of any aromas of soaps and colognes. Almost as angry as the lady, was the technician assigned to make the call. He was the one ranting in the snack room. Now I understood. Poor fellow, how undignified.

Was this a matter of customer satisfaction? Was this a matter that should have been directed to Human Resources or Legal? Did the Manager show good judgment giving in to the customer? I couldn't help but wonder what would have happened if this had been a Sales Rep and a Sales Manager faced with this situation.

Sure enough, I didn't have to wait very long. A couple of weeks later I answered the phone for the Sales Rep that sat next to me when he stepped away from his desk. It was the husband of the lady who had the "odor sensitivity." He requested that a Sales Rep prepare a Sales Contract for a piece of equipment and mail it to their business address where they would sign it and then return it. He went on to admonish that once the equipment was delivered, the Sales Rep coming out to install the equipment must be free of any odors from soap, cologne, etc. By the way, the Sales Rep needed to be "odor free" while preparing the Contract, otherwise the lady would be affected by the scent attached to the paper on which the Contract was prepared.

As soon as the Sales Rep returned to his desk I told him about the call. ("I took a call for you, Pal. The good news is you got a *Bluebird*. The bad news is…".) I explained in great detail the circumstances and the supporting bits of information as best I was able to recall them from the snack room incident.

"We'll just see about that", he said. "I'll go in and talk to the Branch Sales Manager. I'll take this to Corporate."

Can you guess the outcome? How would you have resolved this encounter? In reflection, I am not sure I agreed with the way it was handled, but this is what happened:

The Sales Rep marched in and made his case to the Branch Sales Manager. The Sales Rep expressed his objections in no uncertain terms. He steered the matter out of the realm of business into a personal matter. He was personally offended. To my surprise, the Branch Sales Manager agreed with the Sales Rep without equivocation. The Branch Sales Manager told the Sales Rep that he did not have to acquiesce to the demands of the client since they both felt that the client was being unreasonable. The Branch Sales Manager got right into the thick of things. He called the client, thanked her for being a long-time user of our products and services, and explained how he would not and could not demand that one of his Sales Reps be subjected to her conditions for doing business. The Branch Sales Manager went on to explain that the Sales Rep had rights too, and if he objected to these demands, and he did, then the Sales Rep would not be compelled to accommodate the situation in the prescribed manner. The Branch Sales Manager told the client that he would document their conversation and send a copy of the letter to Headquarters to make his position official. The Customer Service Department was also copied and reprimanded for subjecting the technicians to these demands against their will.

Now, after all that the Branch Sales Manager promised the client that he would actively seek out Reps (Sales and Service) that did not object to these conditions and assign them to her account. He would find some way to reward them for their efforts towards "customer satisfaction" and do his best to be respectful of her needs. On the surface, this seemed to work because the client was ecstatic that a major corporation had bent over backwards to treat her in a special way. Nobody got sued and the client continued to do business with the company.

Do you have any thoughts? Was this Sales Mastery or the proverbial Can of Worms? Perhaps my critique of the Branch Sales Manager was somewhat misguided. After all, everybody got something as the business pipeline continued to flow.

POMP AND CIRCUMSTANTIAL

Whenever someone asks me about my background and experience, I always begin my retort with, "I was born and raised at IBM."

I have worked for a number of companies, but it was Big Blue that made selling my life's work. Even though I never rose to the upper echelon of their corporate structure, I had a pretty good run. That's not to say there weren't some awkward times and events, or that I agreed with all that took place, and I'm not just referring to the wide brim hats and hymnals. That's right, at one time IBMers sang from a corporate hymnal and the Salesmen wore wide brim hats as a part of the expected dress code. Of course, all of this predated my day. In reflection, it's hard for me to believe some of the silliness that I encountered.

One day my Branch Manager told me to get a photo of myself and a short bio together and give them to my Marketing Manager. I did so without question, because it was the Branch Manager that had instructed me to do so. Once I gave the information and photo to the Marketing Manager, of course, my curiosity got the best of me.

"Why do you need this?" I asked.

"Because I am putting together a portfolio in preparation for the visit of some VIPs from headquarters next month," explained my Marketing Manager.

VIPs? Headquarters? What Visit? I didn't get the connection. Seeing the puzzled look on my face, the Marketing Manager explained that whenever VIPs came to the field offices, they wanted to be able to approach the Reps without introductions and address them by their first name and ask about the family, by name.

"You're kidding me, right?"

"I'm not kidding," he said.

I'm not sure what I said next, but I am sure that I must have stuttered. I couldn't help but think of what a convoluted mixture of Pomp and Circumstance this protocol was—and for what? Why was it important for the VIP to know my name and ask about my family when they didn't even know me? Was such pretentiousness really necessary? The thing that caused me the most anxiety was how on Earth were they going to remember all those names, faces, and bios? We had more than 30 Reps in our office at the time.

Before I knew it, the day of the visiting VIPs was upon us. Here they come. Just look at the three of them. Cut from the same cloth, dressed alike, and looking like triplets: one from Sales and Support, one from Maintenance and one from Administration.

"Hi, Bill."

"Robert, how are you?"

"Tom. Good to see you. How's Mary?"

"Bob, how's that big Mag Card deal coming along?"

I did not believe my ears. Uh oh, here they come straight at me. What should I do? How will I react? No matter—they walked right by me and didn't say a word. However, once they got two feet beyond me, it started up again.

"Fred, Bradley, Mel, how are you?" They kept walking straight into the Branch Manager's office.

Well, I think I figured out how they remembered all those names, faces and bios–THEY DIDN'T! They chose a few and committed only those to memory. What a charade.

But wait, there's more...

Later that day, I was called into the Branch Manager's office where he and one of the visiting VIPs were waiting to talk to me. I had no idea why they asked me to meet with them but I thought it was probably related to the super month I had. For the sake of the story, I'll address the visiting VIP as Charlie. I honestly don't remember his name...I never got his bio.

"Charlie and I would like to talk to you about a matter that occurred in your territory, Tyrone," the Branch Manager said. "Now, before we continue, I hope you are going to tell us that this never happened."

Oh, boy...what now? From the sullen look on their faces, I could tell that this was serious. Well, let me have it—what's up?

"Tyrone, one of our customers wrote a letter to headquarters excoriating us for our unfair and unethical business policies and practices. It seems that a comment you made to her is at the center of her dissatisfaction and the motivation for writing the letter."

(Oh, my...I'm not sure I want to hear the rest of this.)

"Boss, I can't imagine what you're talking about."

"The customer alleges that you told her that you were exempt from having to make quota because of our special minority assistance program. Tyrone, please say it ain't so."

At that moment everything and everybody in the room seemed to be getting larger, or I was becoming the Incredible Shrinking Man. I attempted several uncomfortable "uhs and ahs" before collecting my wits enough to make a stab at reconciling. Fact is, I was unusually out of sorts because there was some truth in what the customer had charged.

"Please let me explain. That's not exactly what happened," I said trying to be businesslike and calm. Here's the real story (and I'm sort of sticking to it):

I had an account located in one of the more rural industrial parks that represented some substantial potential for equipment purchases. I spent a lot of time and energy trying to become their vendor of choice for office products. I made several presentations and demonstrations and provided them with loaners, and I was about as responsive as I could be, to no avail. After a while, it began to appear that the customer's refusal to buy from me was somewhat unreasonable and maybe even irrational. I just couldn't seem to please them. I employed several wicked "pencil sell" justifications and provided references of some nearby companies with similar buying criteria.

One day (at the end of a very long day) I decided to make them the last call and ask for their business one more time. I remembered some old sales adage about 80% of sales being done after the fifth time the Rep asked for the order, but only 20% of all Reps asked more than three times. Well, I was not going to be a victim of that statistic (even if I was not sure of the exact percentages). Failure to get them as a customer was not going to be as a result of my lack of effort. I confronted the decision maker with a mild variation of the assumptive close—

"Well, how many shall we schedule in your initial shipment?"

"Well, actually...none," she said. "We have decided to go with one of your competitors and we already placed an order for the first shipment, earlier today."

I was floored! It was all I could do not to show how disappointed I was in her proclamation. And that's exactly how she delivered the news of their decision. Here is a frozen moment in time that only a Sales Rep could appreciate—it was the look on her face. That wicked grin as she informed me of their course of action. I know customers buy from people they like, but what do you do when they don't like the way you look, the way you talk, the way you dress, the way you...? What if they don't like anything about you? These were the thoughts now racing through my mind. That's why they had been such a difficult sell. They simply didn't like me.

So, while I was firmly rooted in a defensive mode, I said to her, "Well you know, that's okay. I'm covered under a special quota attainment program at IBM. The minority Reps are not required to sell as much as the other Reps. Yea, I'll be fine. In fact, I have already made quota for the year. I'll be celebrating at the 100% Club in Miami next March."

Then I faded into the woodwork as did the grin on her face. No sooner had I gotten to my car and I began to regret what I had done. Not only had I been dishonest, I had sunken to being mean-spirited. Tit-for-Tat. She became the Wicked Witch from the North and I went from thirty-something to nine years old. But I simply could not help myself. I am telling you, it was that look on her face—that vindictive look that some customers get when delivering bad news to Sales Reps. If you stay in Sales long enough, I guarantee you, one day you'll get that look.

Some time had passed and I pretty much had put the incident behind me until the confrontation in the Branch Manager's office.

"So, you don't have to make quota, huh?" one of them said. They seemed to agree that the only thing more ridiculous than my remark was the fact that the customer believed that IBM had such a policy.

After about 15 minutes, or so, of reprimand they admonished me to never repeat this sort of thing again and make sure that I didn't share this story with any of the other Reps. I agreed and apologized again. I got up and slowly walked out of the office. As I closed the door, I heard them laughing out loud. They could hardly wait for me to leave the room. I didn't dare go back. I quietly stood on the other side of the door listening to them roar.

I was at my desk when the VIPs departed. I couldn't help but hear the mock ritual.

"Okay Tom, best of luck."

"George. Jim. Knock 'em dead."

"See you in Miami, Bill."

Just then, one of the VIPs looked at me as he was going out the door and said, "Oh, Tyrone. Give my best to Susan." (That was the name of the person who wrote the letter.)

FUNNY, SAYS WHO?

There is another bit of silliness that occurred while I was at Blue about which I feel somewhat compelled to say a word or two. Now, you may not think this is so significant, but it caused a lot of emotions and feelings to be stirred. Let me set the stage a bit.

Fierce competition had forced a major overhaul of the Office Products Division. The 'brain trust' decided to split the Division into two groups. One group (Office Products) would sell typewriters, copiers, and small electronic typewriters. The other group (Office Systems) was to sell dictation systems, word processing equipment, and communications products that interfaced with the computer. The Office Systems group was hailed as the "Chosen One." Supposedly these were the Reps with the technical and business acumen to present and close the more conceptual sale. In fact, most of that group considered the move to be a step-up in prestige and organizational clout. But not all of the 'gifted ones' chose to go over to the other side and sell Office Systems. Most of the old-timers stayed with the Office Products group. That group was doing extremely well and there was no reason to leave.

Well, it didn't take long for the Office System group to begin to fall flat on its face. Competitors like Xerox, WANG, NBI and CPT were handing them their proverbial heads on a Mylar Platter. No sales group at Blue had ever done so badly and the fact that the Office Products group was doing so well caused visible consternation between the two.

This all came to a head at a Regional Product Announcement Meeting. Our Branch Office was asked to perform a business skit to help launch the new product. Since no script was provided, one of our more fun loving Reps with a quick wit and a keen sense of humor took it upon himself to create the skit. After two brief and incomplete rehearsals back at the Branch, we all thought the skit was a satirical masterpiece—clever lines, funny situations, and a great wrap-up that ended with a demonstration of the product. What followed; however, was a debacle.

As we were performing the skit, we could see the discomfort on the faces of the audience in the first few rows. We finished the skit, but instead of the standing ovation that we expected, there was but a mere polite applause. Heck, what was that all about? We soon found out...

The Regional Manager took the podium to wrap-up the announcement. He was visibly shaken. He managed to get through it but not without letting us all know that the skit was inappropriate. *(Aw, man! No way, that skit was funny!)* Unfortunately, it didn't end there.

The Meeting ended around the lunch hour and our Branch Manager asked all Reps to meet back at the Branch at 2:00 p.m. for a brief Sales Meeting. By the time we all gathered, the Branch Manager was behind closed doors. Word was he was being chewed a new one by the Regional Manager. It seemed as though a group of the Office Systems people had mounted a complaint campaign in objection to our skit. They went directly to the Regional Manager and asserted that the skit was unprofessional, inappropriate and offensive. WOW, they were truly wounded! The Branch Manager appeared in the hallway looking relatively unscathed in light of all that had happened.

He positioned himself in the middle of the sales floor and said, "Gang you won't believe the earful I just got from the Regional Manager."

He shared some of the conversation then somebody shouted, "It's those no good malcontents from Office Systems that are agitating the Regional Manager! They're just jealous because we're doing so well and they can't sell their way out of a wet paper bag!"

We all agreed but we were still having trouble trying to figure out what in particular was so awful about our skit. The Branch Manager went on to explain that they felt our use of colloquial humor was out of place and that the Black Reps were offended by my use of a southern dialect to deliver one of my lines. And, if that weren't enough, the ultimate sacrilege was the making fun of one of the products. The entire office was in a gasp. No, no, no, I thought to myself. I am just not going to give in to that nonsense. The skit was done in fun and didn't hurt anyone.

The saga continues…

The next day we found out that the Regional Manager actually fired our Branch Manager. The Reps quickly mounted a mass mailing to headquarters in hopes of heading off this catastrophe. The Branch Manager was about as cool as he could be.

When he realized what we were doing, he again came to the sales floor and said, "I appreciate what you're doing but it's really not necessary. If they'll fire me over this, then maybe I don't need to work here."

Well, all right! The Branch Manager was a Master Chef who always wanted to go back to California and open his own restaurant, anyway. I always respected the way our Branch Manager handled this situation, and I was also pleased with how I held my ground. The Branch Manager was reinstated and there were no official reprimands or punishments meted out, and we all lived happily ever after—sort of…

Although I was thoroughly convinced that this episode was brought about as a result of some professional jealousies, and that our group didn't deserve the angered criticisms that were hurled at us, I must admit that it had a profound effect on my corporate conditioning.

Both of the aforementioned events took place in the '70s. I have not participated in a skit of any kind since that day and in places where I have had approval or authority over whether a skit was performed or not, I have not allowed it. I don't tell jokes (ethnic or otherwise), and I am extremely conscious of how I refer to, respond to, and am in contact with people in the business setting. Nothing I say or do in the business world will ever be misconstrued, misrepresented, or misinterpreted, again! But, that's not to say I can't be funny from time-to-time…

June 2, 1978

Mr. Frank Cary
Chairman of the Board
IBM Corporation
Old Orchard Road
Armonk, New York 10504

Dear Mr. Cary:

I joined this company in 1971 as an installer for the Bethesda
Office of the Office Products Division. I worked for two
years as an installer. During this time, I simply fell in
love with this company. I not only enjoyed my job, but I
enjoyed the people as well. And uppermost, I felt that the
high ideals of this company set it head and shoulders above
all the rest. When I was offered a job as a salesman, I
jumped at it. You would have had to go down a long list of
names to find one who thought more of this company than
myself. I merely wish that I could say the same in 1978.

In my opinion there have been any number of bad business
decisions made over the past few years. But, I never formally
complained. I simply beared down and tried to do the best
job I could. I have tried to leave the decision making to
those paid to make the right decisions. However, on May 31,
1978, Jerry ▓▓▓▓ was removed as Branch Manager of the
Office Products Division, Bethesda Office. I cannot sit by
and let such a grossly unfair act go unchallenged. This
letter is my attempt to bring your attention to a matter
which so desperately needs some sane reasoning.

If this letter brings reprisal, then so be it. The job that
Jerry ▓▓▓▓▓ has done toward making this office the best in
the region deserves more than a slap in the face like this.
Bethesda needs Jerry ▓▓▓▓▓.

Truly disheartened,

Tyrone L. Cypress
Marketing Representative
Office Products Division

mh

(Illustration XII)

WHAT'RE YOU LOOKING AT?

I've had a number of *OJT* experiences that have had a profound effect not only on my career but all aspects of my life. I have trouble relating the events of this specific experience in any meaningful way because it was so bizarre. In my attempt not to identify certain people and companies by name, I find myself dancing around the crux of the experience when attempting to tell the story. Furthermore, the lack of detail sharing also tempers my ability to expound on the lessons learned. Let's see if this makes my point.

One day I got a call at the office informing me that a fellow Rep from out-of-town had sold a substantial machine order in his territory but it was being shipped to my territory. HOT DOG! During those days, the "Ship To" Rep got 75% of the Sell Credit. I got the contact information and called the company President to arrange for the installation of the machines (typewriters) when they arrived. I thought it was a bit unusual for an out-of-town order to be delivered to a headquarter location, but oh well. Since I didn't even know the account was there, 75% of the order was just fine with me.

I explained to the President that a Representative from our company had to unpack the equipment and install it or the warranty would be voided. I decided that this would be a good time to meet Mr. Big and maybe sell him some additional products, so I went out to do the installs myself.

I got there early in the morning and was directed to the machines. I went about my business and then noticed that one of the machines was missing. When I inquired as to its whereabouts, I was told that it was in the President's office. Well great, I'll finally get a chance to meet him. I was escorted to the President's office where the receptionist knocked on the door and announced my arrival. Then she walked away. The door was locked but I could hear the sound of hardware clanking. He opened the door just enough for me to squeeze in and I was told to "Enter." Although the door was on the main level, there was a six foot flight of stairs directly behind the door and when I entered I couldn't help but notice the room was very dark. (Good grief, what is this all about?) Things brightened a little as I got to the top of the stairs, but it was only the light from the monitors and the electronic devices in the room. But, these weren't computer monitors, they were T.V. monitors. To my amazement, the President had T.V. monitors showing every employee's workstation and every employee as they went about their work. This was an electronics assembly and sales company and Mr. Big explained to me that the urge to pilfer was too great to ignore. He had to keep an eye on each 'company asset.' One thing that was very clear was that he didn't merely look in on his employees periodically, he monitored them constantly. His office was a command post where he sat each day overlooking the troops and their work. Ironically, I was there for almost an hour and he never completely looked away from his bank of monitors. He never looked me in the eye. He would talk to me while observing the screens, occasionally diverting his attention to a pad of paper where he made notations from time to time.

Since the light was so low, at one point I asked if he would like me to take the machine outside the office to unpack and assemble.

"Oh no, please do it here," he said.

He stood behind me the entire time and expounded upon multiple business axioms while I unboxed the unit and took it through the installation routine. Some made sense and some didn't. When I had finished, he invited me to have a seat while he told me all about the company—what they did and their various successes.

As I said, "Good-bye," and made my way down the stairs and out the door, I couldn't help but wonder if he was watching me on the monitors as I left the building. The cameras mounted on the walls were very visible all over the building. What about the parking lot?

This incident troubled me for a long time. However, I never talked about it to anyone and since I lost the account in a territory change (and there weren't anymore out-of-town purchases), I never called on him again. I concluded that I had been privy to a bad case of voyeurism that didn't warrant any further attempts at reconciliation or justification.

TEACH AND PREACH—MY TURN

Without a doubt, the most enjoyable experience of my sales career was the time I spent as a Guest Instructor at IBM Sales School. At 'Blue' it was well known that being selected to go to Dallas as a Guest Instructor meant that you were being considered for a major move up the corporate ladder and of course, the selected few were recognized as the best of the best Sales Reps. Man, what a stroke. With so many terrific Reps all vying for upward mobility, a successful stint in Dallas was a real separator.

I found that the toughest battles I endured while trying to make my way in that awful 'rural patch' a.k.a. assigned territory, for the last few years had actually prepared me quite well for the tasks and assignments presented to me as an Instructor. In fact, in reflection, I found the whole thing to be somewhat easy, and I managed to do extremely well—as indicated by my performance rating and remarks of the School Executives.

I am sure, in part, that things seemed to come rather easily because I had so much fun and thoroughly enjoyed working with all of the young, bright students. They were eager to benefit from the frontline experiences of a successful Rep and hung on my every word. After all, in the backdrop of every lesson or recommended technique, there was an aura of "been there, done that." Almost as rewarding were the bragging rights afforded when returning to the Branch to share the experiences with my coworkers; and there were many about which to talk. Perhaps one day I'll write another book telling all about the events of my Guest Instructorship—many facets, many dynamics, and many personal and professional sagas. I could easily devote several chapters to each individual student—their interpersonal relationship with me, with other students, and with other faculty. Not to mention my own episodic adventures.

You know, I think it was this endeavor that ultimately led to my repressive urges to become a teacher one day once I have retired from my active Sales career. I use the term 'repressive' because I find myself reacting to those who see teaching as a profession for those who can't compete in the real world, i.e., *"Those who can—do. Those who can't—teach."* I'm not sure of the origin of that little dig, but I have certainly heard it plenty of times. I suppose one sure sign of maturity is being able to pursue one's happiness without being derailed by other's criticisms and negative castigations.

I must admit, that over the years, I have probably been susceptible to more than my share of what others think. It seems that nearly every aspect of my life has come under attack in one way or another. My attire, the company I keep, the way and on what I spend my money, even the cars I drive. Too flashy, too conservative—"he must be trying to compensate for some sort of deficiency." Fortunately, I have gotten past that phase of my life. My happiness is just that...

August 23, 2005

Dear Whomever,

Take your best shot!

Sincerely,
Mr. Resolved
Mr. Resolved

Mr. Tyrone Cypress
IBM Corporation
4350 East West Highway
Bethesda, MD 20014

R. H. ██████
Staff Instructor
OP Marketing Training
September 2, 1977

Dear Tyrone,

Congratulations on being chosen to be a guest instructor at
Marketing Training. I am looking forward to working with you
during two very important weeks of the Basic School curriculum.

During our phone conversation, we discussed the enclosed
article. The information contained in this article should
be presented in a 30-minute class discussion. We also
discussed a second presentation. This presentation should
not exceed 45 minutes. The major objective of this presentation is to ensure that the students are able to utilize
your sales idea upon their return to the branch. Some
suggestions for preparing these presentations would include:

o   Keep it simple. They are new hires, not experienced
     Sales Representatives.

o   Encourage two-way discussion.

o   Include an exercise or some way to ensure they are able
     to use your idea.

o   Include a handout.

Prior to your arrival at Marketing Training, please review
the Rules and Business Conduct sections of your PAR Manual.
During your stay at Marketing Training, students will ask
you many questions regarding disparagement and unhooking.
It is imperative that you be familiar with this information
and can answer all questions accurately.

(Illustration XIII)

Mr. Tyrone Cypress
September 2, 1977
Page 2

Also, please review the Preschool Training Guide, Volumes 59,
80, and 81, in the Marketing Reference Library. This new
training guide will give you an overview of Basic School as
it exists today and, in addition, give you an idea of the
eight-week preschool training received by the students with
whom you will be working. This review should also include
viewing the video, "Making of a Professional" (Training
Volume 1, Marketing Reference Library). This will give you
an excellent overview of what you will be seeing while at
Marketing Training.

During their preschool training, the students are required
to view the Basic Selling Skills volume located within the
Branch Offices. To ensure continuity of terminology and
concepts, please review all six modules in this VTR with
special emphasis on modules two, three, and four. The work-
book should also be completed for further reinforcement
of this information.

If you have any questions, please call me at ▮▮▮▮▮▮▮
▮▮▮▮▮▮▮▮▮▮▮▮▮▮▮▮▮▮▮▮▮▮. I am looking
forward to meeting and working with you.

Sincerely,

LP07

cc: ▮▮▮▮▮

(Illustration XIV)

COZY SALES 'COUPE'

Outside sales—now that's for me. Give me my quota and assigned territory and point me. That's the only way to go. I really enjoyed the "ride time" while making joint calls with other Reps. *There's nothing like the smell of two or more Reps in the morning on their way to that first call.* More than hanging, better than bonding, I liken it to 'congregationalizing'. These trips provide fertile opportunities for learning, socializing, philosophizing, venting, and pontificating…And people who were not necessarily cut from the same cloth—all the better. Let's all get in the car and go.

Not too long ago I was on my way to a product demonstration with three other *Consultants*. We decided to take one car to save on expenses and hassles. For a brief moment I thought the infamous Beltway commute would provide a chance for some real sales talk and business banter. Not two minutes into the ride my cell phone rang. I only talked for a moment, but before I hung up one of the other guys' phone rang. Before long, all four of us were on our phones and there was never a moment when at least one of us was not on the phone.

Efficiency…Productivity…OH, PLEASE! I know, but do we always need to be in touch with something or somebody? I am aware of the power of a myriad of wireless devices and convinced that they are necessary tools of our trade, but I still long for the good ol' days.

Those were the good ol' days and I miss them dearly. I refer to those times as the good ol' days because times have changed and the ways in which we go about conducting business are different—compunctions, territory coverage, customer service, etc.

MOTIVATE IF I MIGHT

Although most of my sales experience has been spent in management, my style, methodology and approach to the Selling Game has evolved from real-world events and encounters mitigated in the trenches—undoubtedly shaping my perspective. From my point of view, that is a significant rejoinder. I think it's fair to say that I am highly unorthodox in how I interpret and respond to the nuances of the business world. More than likely that is because the world of business and the approach necessary to be successful is a living, ever evolving thing. We learn, we grow, we apply. Depending on how much we learn and how much we grow, dictates how we apply what's been learned.

For example, I have absolutely changed my views on motivating my Sales Reps. Notice I did not say I changed my view on "how to" motivate my Reps—I don't even try to motivate them. (I can just see the eyebrows arching.) I have become thoroughly convinced that only a gifted few are truly able to motivate people. The rest of us should not even try. I am well aware of the different arguments on how to instill fear and engage in games that tug at the various emotions of a Rep, but I think those methods are only superficial attempts that in the end produce only marginal results. Motivation does not scare a Rep into producing.

I remember an occasion when I called a Rep into my office to discuss why his numbers had nose-dived so drastically and what we could do to turn things around. Well, it didn't take long for the spirit of this little tête-à-tête to begin to unfold.

"Why has there been such a lack of progress in bringing in the business?" I barely had time to ask.

The Rep crossed his arms and legs, leaned back in his chair (unmistakable body language) and said, "I'm just not motivated."

It was another frozen moment in time. Although there was only a second or two that went by between his comment and my reply, it was incredible how much passed through my mind during that schism.

He was not motivated? Why not? Was I supposed to motivate him? Was this a legitimate reason?

In this nanosecond, I grasped, consumed, weighed and decided I was being conned. It was a moment that altered my perspective.

"Joe,[1] let me get this straight. Are you saying that I am responsible for your motivation to perform?

With arms and legs still crossed, Joe did not respond.

"Well, how do we get you motivated and whose responsibility is it to provide that motivation?"

"Uh, I don't know. I am just not motivated," he said.

Becoming somewhat agitated, I said, "Sorry my man, but that won't work." I dismissed him and told him to meet with me at the end of the day to discuss a 90-day plan for improvement.

What I wanted to say was, *"Joe, it is not my responsibility to provide your motivation. Motivation comes from within you, not within me. As a professional it is up to you to muster up the necessary stamina and moxxy to sustain a successful effort. Blaming someone else for your lack of motivation is a copout!"*

As far as I am concerned there is only one way to drive a sales force and that is through the use of incentives. I make a comprehensive effort to fully explain the sales plan and get reassurances from the Reps that they understand how they will be remunerated based on their achievements at every level—Here's the plan: Make it and you get "X", miss it and you don't. It's

---

1. Names have also been changed to protect "Joe"

motivation by default. The incentive is the motivator. Basic as it may seem, it's served me well.

For personal motivation I have found two rather unconventional (and until now, secret) ways to summon up my spunk and get my motivational juices flowing. They are as follows:

1. Tune into the "Wildlife Channel" and view an episode on hyenas. The harsh reality of their existence and challenge to survive seems to jolt the silliness and fluff right out of me. Grow up! Nature's covet is aggression.

2. Early in the morning, drive to a "bad" part of town, park my car and board a local commuter bus at its first stop. Stay on until the end of the line, get off and board the next bus back to my car. For maximum effect, I do this in inclement weather. Mingling with people who have to *work for a living* is the ultimate Course Corrector.

Get busy! You have abilities so use them.

GOTTA GROW

As a Sales Manager, I would constantly find myself in the role of a prospect. Many Reps selling a wide range of products and services would call on me. I always enjoyed being the customer. I never minded the repeated phone calls requesting appointments for demos and presentations. If I had the time to see 'em, I would and if not, I would politely ask them to be in touch at a later date.

I used to compare the various styles and approaches of the Sales Reps calling on me. I would actually pick-up a trick or two in the process. I had a chance to observe up close and personal, a full range of skills and techniques.

I once got a call from a Rep whose company provided Sales Training and referenced a significant amount of success with both large and small companies all across the Country. Even though I had never heard of them, I was impressed with his canvassing effort.

"Yea, come on by. Show me what you got."

(FAST FORWARD)

"Tyrone, your 10:00 a.m. appointment is here," announced the receptionist.

"I'll be right down."

As I approached the lobby, I could see that there was only one person in the waiting area but this could not be the gentleman calling on me. He was dressed in business attire, but he was wearing a turban. After a lightning fast once over, I became fixated on his turban. (A turban? No, no, no…Is this a put-on? He must be kidding…) these were the days of the conservative dress code for outside Sales Reps. I tried to be as polite as I could and asked him to follow me to my office.

"I hope you're not put off by my turban," he said.

He could see that I was preoccupied with the turban and this was his attempt to squelch my obvious anxiety. I couldn't help but think that this is how it must have been in my early days at IBM when I had a big Afro and would catch customers talking to my hair.

Let us proceed to the "Land-o-Lamnity"—Frankly, it didn't matter much what he said, I simply could not get past the turban. I can't remember more than four or five words of his spiel; I don't remember how we *wrapped-it-up* or what our next step was; but I do remember never doing business with him.

Over the years, I have become very familiar with the company represented by the 'Rep with the Turban'. The company was a franchised operation made up of a group of gritty, pure sales types. In retrospect, I believe I missed an opportunity to grow professionally. I often refer back to this event to temper my perspective regarding how to evaluate potential opportunities. I now make it a point to LOOK BEYOND THE TURBAN...

THAT'S THE U Δ ME

Perhaps the biggest paradox in Sales Management for me has been the mere selection process. Who is the best candidate for Sales Management? Here again, you might think my views are somewhat warped, but it has been my experience that the best Salespeople are promoted to Management. (HUH?) Am I the only person that thinks that this is nonsensical?

What about the notion of keeping your best sales performers in the field where they are productive? I'll concede that this is a debatable point but my experiences shape my views. Good Sales Reps don't necessarily make good Sales Managers. Promote them at your own risk. The argument against this concept is that you must promote your top performers into management or you will lose them and they will go elsewhere to gain a position in management. However, time and time again, I have seen the top Reps promoted into Management only to become mediocre. Consequently, the company suffers from the void created by removing a top sales performer from the territory.

Doesn't it make better sense to create an environment and *comfort zone* for top Salespeople to perform and be rewarded so that they don't have to feel compelled to go into Management? Traditionally, we squeeze the productive life right out of the top performers. After a successful year, we shrink their territories and increase their quota.

I once had a Rep say to me, "My goodness, Tyrone. I don't mind you asking me to jump the umbrella, but don't hoist it while I am in mid-air."

This was a rather esoteric retort but I got the message.

More often than not, good Sales Reps go into management just to escape the madness. All too often, Sales Managers are forced into multi-tasking and required to perform Sales and Administrative duties in addition to all the other things they do. Once an organization has either been good enough or lucky enough to acquire a top sales performer, why would they then take them out of the field and inundate them with adminis-trivia—requiring them to be babysitters, shrinks, counselors, and people problem solvers? I know that these can be important elements of good leadership but shouldn't someone other than your best Sales Rep handle them?

Companies that encourage tops Sales Reps to stay in the field are rare—a fact that still puzzles me after 30 years. Imagine being able to just sell, sell and sell. A bit idealistic? Well, judging from how things have been done in the real world over the years, I guess it is. Traditional thinking prescribes to the notion that by putting a top sales performer in charge of other Sales Reps that it will in some way 'rub off'—that ain't necessarily so. In fact, I am here to testify that just the opposite is likely to occur. The usual order of events is that a top Sales Rep is promoted (squeezed) into Sales Management where he or she becomes totally frustrated and Reps flounder under his or her management.

Case in point: Why don't more top athletes become managers during their MVP year, not after retirement, but during their prime? It's my con-tention that this should apply to the business world as well. The transition, if desired, should be facilitated, not forced, when the time is right.

Believe it or not, the most enjoyable Sales Manager for whom I have worked couldn't sell worth a darn. In fact, his corporate claim to fame was that he was known as "The Guy Who Microwaved His Soup While It Was Still in the Can"...(The explosion traumatized a number of the staff for days.) So what was his strong suit? He looked the part. He was the epit-ome of a confident, successful executive. Tall, broad-shouldered, and blessed with an 'FM Radio' voice. He reminded me of Bruce Wayne, a.k.a. Batman, whenever he spoke. No matter what he said, the decibel level never changed: "Well *Ta-rone*, I guess you'll just have to turn it up a notch," was said with the same amount of enthusiasm as "What a spar-kling performance. I guess all that hard work really paid-off, big time."

This Manager had one trait that I truly admired and I have met very few people who have a real command of it. This guy had the ability to take questions from an audience, repeat the questions in their entirety, and then answer. You think that's easy? He did it flawlessly, no matter how long or multifaceted the question.

"But was he effective?" you ask. His *'managerialship'* worked for me. His sales teams were always among the company's leaders. Arguably, I contend a sales force can be successful in spite...

WHO'S ETHICS?

I was a Sales Manager at a small office products company with a sales force of 10 Reps and their territories were split up geographically. One of the Reps covered a section of the downtown area where a 'striptease joint' was located. Well, this was a very large business that needed office products, too. Sure enough they called the office and asked if a Sales Rep could come out and take an order for some office equipment (a Bluebird). The message was channeled to the Rep but instead of going to the establishment to handle the order, the Rep got one of the other Sales Reps to go to the customer and consummate the deal. When I got wind of how this deal was handled, I gave the Sell Credit to the Rep who actually went downtown to get the order.

The incumbent Rep was furious with me and thought I was being a real S.O.B. He tried to explain that he was a very religious person of significant status in his church (Jehovah's Witness) and could not in good conscious enter such a facility or even be seen in front of the building. The Rep and I had a very pointed discussion and the Rep left my office no doubt very bitter.

My position at the time was based on a solid conviction that if the Rep was not bothered by the Sell Credit and commission then he should not be so put-off by having to go to the facility to pick-up the order. I found his logic to be hypocritical. After all, I was the Sales Manager and I had the last word!

Although we never talked about it again, I know the Rep never forgave me. To him, my reaction was a belittlement of his faith and church. How ironic that in reflecting on this incident, I'm not sure I made the right call. I'm not sure my rationale was so solid. In fact, I am sure that today I would opt for another course of action. Why hadn't I thought of some creative way to compensate both Reps? Hadn't I been a bit insensitive? Was my reaction the uncovering of some latent phobia of his 'unconventional' beliefs? I had always taken great pride in the way I handled my Reps as a Sales Manager, but this was not one of my highlights.

For a long time afterwards, when I discussed this situation with others, especially other Managers, I would do so in the abstract—never revealing the identity of the people involved. I found it to be of little comfort that most expressed opinions in agreement and support of my initial reaction. I believe I made a mistake.

During a round table discussion at the local *Inn of the Attitudinal Adjustment,* one of my colleagues suggested that this was really no big deal. He went on to conclude that any Sales Manager who thought about this for more than a moment or so was harboring some deep-seeded psychological issues. (I beg your pardon!) How would you have handled the situation?

90...60...80...70...75...SOLD!

The rigors of the profession can truly make one wonder why? What is it that draws so many of us to the challenges of Professional Sales? Is it the moneymaking potential? Maybe, but that's too simple. Fact is, in a Professional Sales career, it is not unusual for a Sales Rep to have long droughts and only modest earnings over the long haul. Now, I won't presume to speak to the motives of all Sales Reps, but here's my offering on the subject.

In a word, it's the "DEAL"—part bartering, part bickering. The back and forth, give and take, then on to the ultimate resolution. This action taps into and latches onto the sheer essence of our personalities. For those of us who'll admit it, and for those who won't, we just love it. The prospect of being at the center of making a deal gets us up in the morning, keeps the midnight oil aflame, and serves as the fuel to energize the prolonged efforts to the 'close'.

What are these magnetic properties of the deal? In a polite discourse, the operative term is *WIN-WIN*. I suppose in the long-term that certainly makes good business sense—repeat business, and all. However, take it from one who has observed the process from all angles, that's not the light that lures us to the bulb. I'll even go so far as to say (I know this is going to be an unpopular utterance.) most Sales Reps don't care one bit whether the deal creates a win-win scenario or not. Sales Reps like to operate within the creases of the hidden agenda or slight of hand. This compelling sense of control, being the center of attention, and the illusion of wielding power, now that's the hook. We are reeled into the action much like a gambler with an addiction. That, at least in part, explains why most Sales

Reps have such a hard time perfecting the process. We get greedy! We leave money on the table. We show, hold and fold all at the wrong times.

Sales Reps in the pursuit of crafting their skills have created an industry unto itself. Just go to the library or any bookstore and you'll find an endless selection of books, tapes, movies and magazine articles on The Deal. Which ever it is, art or science, I have concluded I don't care what you call it. A deal is a deal and a sale is a sale. The necessary preparation to become a successful arbiter may be rooted in any number of disciplines.

The one thing that has always stuck with me though, is the ability to negotiate. This tends to separate the pros from everybody else. Practically every Rep will tell you that negotiating is what they do best. Rookies will tell you that they come by it naturally, and old-timers will bring you to the verge of tears with stories of how they have crafted their skills. Of course, some of us are better than others, but I am not sure how much of one's ability to negotiate in a sales setting comes about naturally. I have observed, however, that the professionals that negotiate best have mastered a technique wherein they are able to remove *ego* from *nego*tiate. This tempered process is a joy to watch. I have been privileged to be on sales calls where I would have paid the price of admission to witness the mastery in action. Dog-gone-it, a polished, knowledgeable, poised, well-groomed, mild-mannered, sincere, prepared, and on time Sales Rep could sell me anything.

Absorb and incorporate—now that's the way. Let's get it right! A delicate balance of knowing when to talk and when to listen, never interrupting, and not too longwinded in either the presentation or response. I am not sure why some Reps feel they have to talk without pausing or permitting anyone else to get in a point or two, but I can attest to the prevalence of just such situations. I have seen Reps talk their way right out of the sale—and never realize it.

If it seems as though there is no reason or rhyme or if there are contradictions inherently laced in the answer to "Why do we do it?", then that just means we have come full circle. The power of Sales compels us...the power of Sales compels us...the power of Sales compels us.

Throughout this rhetorical endeavor I have tried to present some thoughts and ideas etched into my soul over the years. Consistent with my theme to put forth a "how come" instead of a "how to" version of events, I hope this work is of some value. I have purposely tried to stay away from extreme pontification from on high, because quite frankly, the burden of being the purveyor of sales wisdom is more than I can handle. I am just your everyday Sales Pro trying to make my way. Telling "how to" demands that you must always be right. The trouble with always being right is that you can never be wrong. I don't ever want to be boxed into that world.

Well, that's my story. I have finally got it off my chest. Most of the anecdotes and occurrences recounted in this book are things that I have savored for decades. Aspersions about my chosen profession (and incessant prodding from my wife) have inspired me to dedicate my time and effort to authoring this refrain.

On a good day or not, when contemplating the worth and value of my career choices, let this be known for sure—I can look into the eyes of any inquirer or doubter and without hesitation

SAY IT LOUD...I SELL AND I'M PROUD!

This Page Left Blank Intentionally

978-0-595-38050-3
0-595-38050-6

www.ingramcontent.com/pod-product-compliance
Lightning Source LLC
Chambersburg PA
CBHW030813180526
45163CB00003B/1261